Desires of the Heart:

The Evolution of an American Psychiatrist

William F. Kenny, MD, FAPA

Desires of the Heart: The Evolution of an American Psychiatrist
by W. F. Kenny, MD, FAPA

Subjects: biography, medicine, mental health, psychology, psychiatry.

Design and publishing
Petra Books 2025
petrabooks.ca

8" x 10"
Times New Roman 11/14
Gill Sans 10, 16
ca. 44,000 words
Illustrations
50 lb paper
108 pages

Kenny on therapy

"The art of medicine requires a large dimension of time at leisure…Patients need time to unravel from their daily cares and anxieties. The doctor needs time to focus on the deep realities of the person."

"…I needed to unearth what was most precious and most protected."

"I begin to identify with my patient's experiences and share their pain. Through this process of mutual identification, we begin to exorcise our shared demons. It is my fight as well. I try to evolve a new and safer reality to replace this haunted dialogue. My task is no less than to fashion a new beginning, a life enriched with meaning."

"Psychotherapy is a two-way street…I found that listening and feeling were more important than advice or direction."

"I seek the truth hidden in the most sensitive desires of the soul, the whispered dreams of long ago. Then I become an intruder who rearranges the landscape and asks to be trusted. I justify the risks and the pain in the hope of a new life free of fear and dread."

Dedication

My Constant Gardener

I see her from the kitchen window as she inhabits her garden.
She is sitting cross legged and bent over white flowers.
I am drawn towards her yet hesitate to invade her private world.
She speaks silently, tenderly, lovingly.
She has found this work an escape from the workaday world.
Her hands delicately touch the petals that surround her.
Does she talk to them? Do they in turn speak to her?
She lifts her head and glances at her work.
She is finished. She is at peace.

Contents

Near and
Hard to grasp is the god
But where danger is
The deliverer too grows strong
In the darkness dwell the eagles
But fearless man remains as he
Must alone before god; simplicity protects
Him
And no weapon needs he and no
Cunning till the time
When god's failure helps

Freidrich Holderlin
1770-1843

For I shall wander under the setting sun
Till timeless embers testify I've won.

—William F. Kenny, 2022

Foreword

Some of us experience extreme emotional pain as we go through life, harmed in childhood growing up with emotionally-impaired parents. Others, born with extremely sensitive emotions, retreat from life. A few find themselves searching for meaning and a way to deal with their emotions and fears. Occasionally someone comes along who alters these experiences and helps provide a positive outlook.

Psychotherapy, and especially psychoanalytic therapy, can often change this trajectory and provide hope and greater self-worth. In my years as a therapist, I have met such people and found them to be sensitive, caring, and longing to be understood. There are many types of therapies and interventions. Some provide listening, understanding, suggestion and support to a patient struggling to find a new perspective on life. For some, the pain is deeper and springs from earliest experiences. Psychoanalytic psychotherapy is a powerful tool to address such pain. It can open a new world, a new understudying of oneself, and the courage to escape the traumas of a damaged childhood. If the therapy goes well, a new self can emerge.

In the latter half of the 19th century the Viennese neurologist, Sigmund Freud, studied the origins of painful symptoms that seemed to have no physical history. He initially used hypnosis as a way of treating apparent neurological disorders. He also used suggestion as a way of encouraging his patients to remember a painful childhood uncovering symptoms of emotional and physical trauma often brought on by damaged parents. Freud explored their dreams which hid painful experiences.

Eventually he was able to resurrect these memories without the use of hypnosis. Instead of putting his patient under hypnotic trance, he urged them to speak freely and without hesitation. He sat behind the patient listening intently as they lay on the couch. He was able then to connect with the meandering thoughts of his patients. Freud had a strong personality and was a powerful and commanding presence. He would often pressure his patient, literally laying his hands on their skull. He believed that early sexual trauma of varying dimensions might be instrumental in a patient's constricted life. Though his theories were often resisted in the field, many followers spread his theories and treatments. In the early part of the 20th century psychoanalytic treatment, as it was called, became a dominant force in the psychiatric treatment of a variety of mental illnesses. Various followers, such as Carl Jung, adopted and modified his treatment.

Harry Stack Sullivan, an influential American analyst, observed that the most important aspect of therapy was the relationship between patient and analyst. As therapy proceeded, he determined that each individual would become a partner in the therapy. For Sullivan, each response became a building block towards a new vision and understanding of self and others. In order to get to this critical point, the analyst offers himself as an intense listener to the analysand's life story with all his or her history of pain and anguish. Often, the patient expects the therapist to magically relieve his or her pain. However, analytic therapy is a restructuring of the personality and pushes for a deeper understanding of the self. Initially the patient is dependent on the analyst or therapist who offers guidance, support and understanding. In response the analysand is able to open up with his or her thoughts, feelings and desires. As this unfolds, an expanding universe and self-confidence emerges enabling the patient to be someone who can truly love and be loved. In its essence this experience is a dialogue of love with a beginning and ending. The patient will have internalized the best parts of his or her analysis and the fundamental belief that they can be truly loved for who they are.

Some individuals have been so traumatized that their inner selves are buried in anguish and despair. They look for magical solutions and often seek unrealistic relationships. The dark hole of early trauma and parental failing undermines any ability for healthy growth. They trust no one and expect only rejection and ridicule. In their hope to connect they often demand unrealistic support from a friend or partner, pushing their relationships to the brink and demanding a love that is not available. Rejection repeats itself and hope seems impossible. They are unable to grasp that this tragic scenario is a replication of early rejections by an unavailable parent. Nevertheless, they cling to what they know and repeat this scenario many times over. Their problem is that to love someone else they would lose the darkness that was their reality and safety. The analyst must confront these issues by insinuating himself or herself into this dilemma as someone who will be there for them. The therapist or analyst must stand fast during this turmoil. He or she must remain a pillar of stability and establish hope. This steadfastness enables the patient to internalize a new reality and to believe that someone is there who cares and will not disappear.

The therapeutic hour has a beginning, middle and end. It starts with the patient relating his symptoms, fears and anguish. It is essential that his or her therapist be an intense listener and sensitive to even minute gestures, pauses and silences. Gradually a bond and trust develop as the therapy moves on to the patient's most painful memories and experiences. The therapist in turn listens compassionately. Eventually the patient senses that the therapist is on their side and has understood his or her pain. This experience offers possibility and meaning. Just as the therapeutic hour has boundaries, there ultimately is an understanding that the therapy eventually must end. It is extremely important that the analysand is able to end their dependence and move on, having internalized their experiences and found new strength going forward with a firm belief in himself or herself.

Introduction

I am 87 years old and looking at the end of the road. Today I find myself struggling to belong in a world that is just beyond my reach. I know there are things that I want to do and yet I find myself pulling back, in a never-ending search of who I am. In spite of this, I am generally in good health and reasonably mobile. There are people I care deeply about, especially my wife and sons. Yet, I remain encapsulated and distant. There is a pandemic just outside the door so I anxiously retreat and allow others to face the world. I worry about myself rather than expressing my love. When I look back over the years, my childhood remains a mystery, more so now. Early on I was troubled with a crippling anxiety and at the same time searching for someone I could hardly imagine. I grew up in a large family of high intelligence and intellectual aspiration, graduated magna cum laude from a Jesuit college and entered medical school in Montréal, Québec. I then went on to an established medical career. Eventually I became a psychiatrist treating a variety of patients, young and old. Their problems mirrored my own struggles for expression and intimacy. They were vulnerable individuals whose pain stunted growth and intimacy. I was there for them and in some way, they were there for me. I was more alive during those moments and cherished this intimacy.

My cousin Frank died recently. He was a year older than I and in reasonably good health. It was a shock and brought home how fragile life is. I'd spent a lot of time with Frank when very young when we dined each Sunday with other cousins at my grandmother's house. Those were blissful experiences full of life and joy. This was especially true during various holidays when families got together and revived old stories and adventures. It always seemed to me that we lived in a bubble of friendship and intimacy that would never end. As the years went by these bonds slowly disappeared. Yet I kept up with Frank over the years though infrequently. We took different paths as we evolved, married and raised families. Recently we got together on a trip to Europe and naturally fell into long discussions of our shared childhood. Frank brought up his own memories of those times when we were young and innocent and free. He was positive, hopeful and looking forward to future travel. He is gone now and the ground breaks beneath me. Such a loss!

My parents were insecure. I inherited many of their limitations and this led to an anxious approach to life. It did not help that I was subjected to Irish Catholicism with its inhibiting fear of almost any form of sexuality; that even sexual thoughts could lead to eternal damnation. This resulted in many trips to the confessional. I graduated from grade school with these clouds hanging over me. However, my experience of high school, college and medical school gradually enhanced my understanding of myself and the world around me. I hesitantly approached young women but remained rather innocent sexually. At the same time, I questioned the Catholicism of my youth exploring philosophical studies that expanded my understanding of the world. For me, the existential philosophers were most important; they gave me hope.

Psychotherapy is a two-way street. It was a unique experience for me and opened the way to deep and lasting relationships. Each patient I saw suffered from a wounded childhood and adolescence, often traumatized by parents who were either smothering or emotionally absent. The early days of therapy stirred fear and anxiety over re-enacting their experiences and for some it was less threatening to remain distant. I found that listening and feeling were more important than advice or direction. Sometimes this would be very confusing for me. One patient had troubled relationships that always ended with resentment and anger. He would recount to me his problems with women who either dominated or belittled him. I would try to encourage him and offer words of advice yet after every meeting, he would send me a letter outlining how little I understood him. I would often feel somewhat hurt and rejected and even bewildered by his response. After several months he left treatment still berating me for my lack of understanding and help. It was only after some time that I came to understand that he was treating me just like his mother had treated him. She was a domineering and narcissistic individual who constantly undermined and criticized him. In our sessions he became the self-centered mother and I the helpless child. I understood then that he needed to keep this relationship going throughout his life. A positive atmosphere resurrected fears that he would lose this terrible, yet longed-for mother.

One of the more rewarding and enlightening moments for me was my experience conducting group therapy for university students. They were extremely bright but frustrated with their lives. As group leader, I focused on the level of interaction and trust in the group. Gradually, these students were able to open up to each other and create an intense and intimate atmosphere. I marveled at their ability, sensitivity and genuine caring. I did not attempt to make interpretations nor give instructions. I trusted their intelligence, understanding and love for each other. In turn, I experienced their need and care for me. I was both an insider yet distant enough to understand their problems and difficulties. When asked how I dealt with the stress of these encounters, I confirmed that it was always a positive experience and that I would rather be in this kind of environment than attending a cocktail party where there is only noise and little intimacy. I miss those times and those lovable students.

Early in my medical career, I had the good fortune to explore such intimacy within the bounds of the psychoanalytic hour. My own analysis, while frustrating, enlarged and supported the courage I needed to explore a world which revealed excitement, warmth and fulfillment. I understood this field to be my true vocation, an opportunity to reach out to others. The sharing of hidden desires and fantasies was liberating, giving me the confidence to form other relationships.

I have always been a vivid dreamer. Recently, I dreamt about a beautiful young blonde nurse whom I met during my psychiatric residency. She was somewhat scattered and timid and when I asked her out, she seemed surprised and somewhat afraid. I did not push the matter and some years later she married one of my roommates, also a psychiatrist who unfortunately died prematurely after a long struggle with multiple sclerosis. In later years, she seemed to find her strengths in Hospice, spearheading the caring of patients in the last days of their illness. In my dream she seemed to be reaching out to me but was unable to make contact. Most of my dreams are fragmented and reflect my inability to connect with women. Looking back, I realize that the women I met were adults and I was the child. I longed for something I did not quite understand. During my psychoanalysis, my dreams became more intense, more vivid, freer. As I lay on the couch these vivid dreams unlocked powerful emotions and desires that I had kept buried for years. I felt anxious and joyful as I contemplated the future.

I met Rebecca at a party. She was blonde, bright and vivacious. I had recently returned from Vietnam and met her through friends. I was surprised that she almost immediately accepted me and we bonded emotionally and physically. She lived quite a distance from the city so I spent weekends with her. It was an idyllic and loving relationship constrained by the fact that she had a long-standing relationship with a married older man who was also her boss. It seemed a bizarre situation but she clung to it. Eventually we parted but I kept her in my heart for many years. It was my first true relationship with a woman and opened the door to my freedom.

Growing up, I longed for someone to understand and love me. During a painful adolescence I ran from anyone who approached me. The closest I could get to a woman was dancing, usually on the pier behind the local ice cream store near our summer beach house; Peggy Lee singing 'Lover" playing on the jukebox. I slowly realized that loving another creates the opportunity to being loved. It sounds simple but is in fact complicated. Most people develop an outward personality that protects them from harm. You have to listen to someone very closely to notice the minute signals that offer a window into the soul of another. Small gestures, a slight smile, a sense of openness, and especially laughter, encourage intimacy. Finding someone to love, to actually understand who they are and their needs for acceptance is the privilege of a lifetime. Once you accept this, life becomes much easier.

Memories and Meaning
by William F. Kenny

Published in *Synergy, Psychiatric Writing Worth Reading.* V22, N9, 2015
Queen's University, Department of Psychiatry

I think back to the earliest memories.

Images of my father playing catch with me merge with later glimpses of him returning home from work. He would usually call at noon to touch base with my mother and then arrive home around 5:00 PM. I remember how much I wanted to please him, show him that I could catch the fastest pitch he could throw at me. His stories were magical and took me into a land of enchantment. In those early years, my father embraced the world and brought laughter into our home.

My mother was the one who was always there, always comforting me during the night. I developed asthma early on and often awakened gasping for breath. She would sit me on her lap, calming me with soothing words as she enfolded me with her arms. Little wonder then that I would scream loudly and vehemently when they left me in the care of a babysitter. I was their first child and, for a while, the focus of all their attention.

I am not sure when and why it all began to change. Certainly the arrival of my younger siblings divided their attentions, but there was something else. A bitterness between my parents surfaced around the time I began school, and it smoldered fiercely over the coming years. My mother gained weight, looked weary, and began to drink. My father grew frustrated and angry. He had always needed to be the center of attention, having been the youngest and very spoiled child in a large Irish family. When I look back now, I can see how this undermined his ability to deal with life's later frustrations. He could not evolve with us as we grew into adolescence, and his need for self-adulation grew even stronger. Eventually, open fighting erupted between my parents. Often, I became the mediator and even protector of my mother.

It seemed that the only thing that gained their attention was my success in school. This was fine with me as it offered a way out. High school and university beckoned and I gradually spent more time away. Upon arriving at medical school in Canada, I faced a foreign country and a different culture. While there, I formed friendships and imbibed the differences. Yet, there remained the ties of home, religion, and upbringing. Further training in New York City sharpened my focus and led me to a residency in psychiatry.

As a young psychiatrist, I strained to make sense of new experiences that challenged old beliefs. The Catholicism I knew was conventional and rigid. The world I was encountering offered new ideas and confusing boundaries. Sexually, I was inexperienced and scared. Eventually, I sought refuge with a group of men who were wrestling with similar problems, and we experimented timidly with our identities and relationships. There were no great insights or changes, but the yearning was there to find a way out.

When the war in Vietnam splashed across America, I was conscripted to fight in that foreign land. I remember arriving at the airfield in Saigon and being terrified. It took some time to become adjusted to the realities of the war, but it began the process of my liberation. While there, I read the existential philosophers, especially Karl Jaspers. His concepts of end points as defining our identities resonated with me (1). The prospect of death and the shortness of life caused me to rethink my values and make the best of my allotted time. I was determined to grab hold of my future as a present reality.

On returning to America, my search quickened. I deepened my philosophical ideas and read more psychoanalytic literature. *If I were to break the stalemate in my life, I decided I would have to undergo my own analysis.*

He was a well-known New York analyst who had written several books. His intellect brought instant respect and calmed my fears. At first, I sat up facing him, and later lay on a couch while he sat behind me. I would leave work three times a week to drive into Manhattan and his Park Avenue office. I remember riding up in the elevator, looking at faces and wondering if any were his patients. Invariably, I would arrive some minutes early and spent time in his reception room imagining what went on behind the closed doors. I would imagine him in his room. It always seemed dark and forbidding. As I sat waiting, there was always the strong desire to please him. When he opened his door, I would be jolted out of my reverie. I was a vivid dreamer who sought instant answers. His silences only spurred my imagination. Sometimes I would reveal these dark images, but not always. Throughout, I cherished his knowledge and benefited from his insights. Most of all, I learned to trust my instincts and embrace my sexuality. For this I am eternally grateful.

However, I never felt that he cared for me. I was looking for the father I lost years ago but could not grasp any hint of feeling in that room. Eventually we had a falling out. I had been seriously ill and was unable to come to his office. Despite this, he insisted on charging me for the times that I missed. I felt hurt and angry but never really confronted him. However, I decided that I had to leave therapy. For all his brilliance, he remained an uncaring man.

I do not remember our last session, but it was several years before I finally relinquished his presence in my mind. I measured my success with his accomplishments. Towards that end I tried to write and organize conferences and meetings; his image took a prominent place in the back of my mind. Recently, I saw a picture of him in the New York Times. He was still active in his field and very involved in teaching. Surprisingly, he looked only a few years older than I. I had always pictured him as older and wondered whether he was still alive. To this day I have difficulty holding my patients accountable for missed appointments. From this experience, I know that they think about me more than they are willing to acknowledge. I also know that the most important issue in therapy is whether I care about them.

I continued reading the psychoanalytic literature. For many years, I was inspired by the teachings of Harry Stack Sullivan (2). His insight that the real work of therapy took place between therapist and patient seemed to equalize the playing field. I focused more on how and why I was reacting to the patient. The British Object Relations School clarified and brought to the forefront the patient as a three-dimensional person and not a bundle of instincts (3). André Green pointed to the dark and hidden soul in each of us. (4) My experience with borderline patients and their frail psyches showed just how damaged people can be and just how desperate their longing. Christopher Bollas (5), in his groundbreaking book, The Shadow of the Object (1989), brought home the need to understand the unspoken emotions that were frozen in time. He, along with Heinz Kohut (6), taught me that understanding, acknowledging, and reacting were the bedrock of therapy. For many years, I believed that my role was that of an impassioned observer of my patients' history, experiences, and dreams. Some responded well to this approach while others offered strong resistance. Ironically, many of the latter did quite well without seeming to accept my formulations of the roots of their problems.

Charlene was a young woman who came to me in great despair. This was many years ago during my first year as a psychiatrist. After an initial and halting history, Charlene became quite silent and remained that way for the next three months. She would arrive on time for the sessions but would not say a word. I tried everything and ended up talking about myself just to fill the time and space. I could sense her great pain and distress but never knew just what she was thinking. It was very painful for me while I struggled in vain to reach her. When Charlene left treatment suddenly and without notice, I felt confused, embarrassed, and futile. After a few months I was able to let go of this strange woman. Then, to my great surprise, I received a short note from her. Charlene apologized for leaving so abruptly and explained she had left for the west coast of the United States and thanked me profusely for helping her in ways that I never truly grasped. She ended by writing that therapy had changed her life dramatically and that she was forever grateful. When I look back and think of others, it seems that my effort to understand and reach out to my patients was the one thing that they needed.

In the last year of my therapy, I met the woman who was to be my wife. We were kindred souls who saw the world as a place to reach for our dreams. Over the years she has been that constant presence in my life, sustaining me in both good and bad times. Her love and understanding has made me feel both special and challenged. She has filled that deep hole in my life while expecting that I be there for her. She needed me to be the man that I always was but could never realize. I had to grow into our relationship and respond to the reality of her love for me. In the process, we built a life and family together that is firm, tender, and lasting. This has given me the platform to embrace the world more openly and with more confidence. I am no longer that small child crying in the night for his mother. There is clarity to my vision. I see other people as they are: fellow travelers on the dusty road. In my work, I am able to approach intimacy yet set boundaries with my patients. This is crucial, since my aim is not to possess the other but rather to set him or her free.

The path to individuality can take a circuitous route. When I started my residency in psychiatry in New York City, I met a fellow resident who changed my life. At that time I was quite alone, shy, and intense. Bob, in contrast, was voluble, outgoing, and joyous. He was full of contradictions: a strict Catholic who would stray and then return to the fold of the Church. We often clashed intellectually, but I was drawn to him and his wide circle of friends. This was a group that looked out onto the world with confidence and verve. In the ensuing years, I became a social animal though still remaining somewhat on the fringe of life. The war in Vietnam and marriage brought inward changes while I gained confidence in my ability to participate in the social flow of life. The friends that I met through Bob have been a constant in my life, and over the years we have celebrated time's passing. I shudder to think what my life would have been if I had never met him. Two years ago this man who was so full of joy and adventure died suddenly of a rapidly disseminated cancer. .

References

(1) K Jaspers, Way to Wisdom: *An Introduction to Philosophy*. New Haven: Yale University Press; 1954.

(2) H S Sullivan, *The Interpersonal Theory of Psychiatry*. New York: Norton; 1953.

(3) R Fairbairn, *From Instinct to Self: Selected Papers of WRD Fairbairn*. Ed, E Fairbairn. Northvale, NJ: Jason Aronson, Inc; 1994.

(4) A Green, *On Private Madness*. London: The Hogarth Press, Ltd; 1986.

(5) C Bollas, *The Shadow of the Object: Psychoanalysis of the Unthought Known*. New York: Columbia University Press; 1989.

(6) R R Lee and J C Martin, *Psychotherapy After Kohut: A Textbook of Self Psychology*. Hillsdale, NY: The Analytic Press; 1991.

Text supplied courtesy of Queen's Quarterly (The Quarterly Committee of Queen's University).

The Hidden Self and Negative Identity
by William F. Kenny

Published in Synergy, Psychiatric Writing Worth Reading. V22, N10, 2015
Queen's University, Department of Psychiatry

I accepted the job as a psychiatrist to students at Queens University with some trepidation; I wondered how I would fit in. My previous experiences with a somewhat older and more disabled population did not easily translate to this new environment. Perhaps these young bright people would find me out of touch. Most importantly, I questioned whether I could bring my experiences as a therapist to this new generation. I am primarily interested in how the past shapes our present reality. I feared the need for instant results and superficial solutions. However, to my surprise, I found my young patients eager to engage in dialogue and to share their stories. I found that they were similar to many patients I have seen in the course of my career as a practicing psychiatrist.

The experience has provided me the opportunity to revisit my own past, both pleasant and painful. I have grown both as an individual and a therapist in the process, for in telling their tales, joy has surpassed pain and I have reclaimed the self I had buried long ago. The reminiscence that follows details my work with five students seen on a weekly or bi-weekly basis. As psychotherapy proceeded, sharp images of former patients provided an engaging chorus and hints of wisdom along the way. I have changed their names and circumstances to protect their privacy.

Despair is a cancer that infiltrates the vulnerable among the student population. It can block progress in profound ways. Many see themselves as outcasts living on the fringes of student life. Depression, self-destructive acts, and suicidal gestures inevitably follow. When I meet them, their history reflects social failure while profound guilt saps all energy and vitality. They are bright and intuitively know this should not be their fate, yet they feel boxed-in and dread the years ahead. In his or her own way they say to me: "If this is all I have to look forward to, I might as well kill myself."

Sara was a sensitive arts student. I had been seeing her for several months and she was beginning to make progress. When I told her how much she had grown, a shadow crossed her face and she looked down, as if embarrassed to hear this. She had done well in her exams and was pursuing her goals. For the first time, she had a clear vision of the future, was excited about her career options, and able to confront her boyfriend without feeling guilty. I could sense her growing confidence and felt it important to visibly celebrate this. Yet she still thought of herself as a frightened little girl. Six months before, this young woman was convinced she was crazy. She was depressed, extremely anxious, could not focus, and had great difficulty navigating the shoals of university life. She had been ready to give up. There were times she thought she was hallucinating. I suggested she take medication to calm down. I told her she was not crazy and could benefit from psychotherapy. I believed that she lacked confidence and underestimated herself. In her dreams, she was overlooked and unheard; childhood memories evoked loneliness and despair; she had no sense of herself as a person.

Philip was a fourth-year student in an arts program who was deeply depressed and on high doses of two antidepressants, having recently changed courses due to failing grades. I reduced his medication and suggested psychotherapy. He was very bright and longed for a new direction in life. Philip's father – a man who had settled for a job that eventually consumed him – had berated and belittled his son throughout childhood. Philip's mother was a loving presence pushed into the background. Philip had hoped to avoid his father's fate, but was uncertain of his own future.

He proved to be an articulate and vivid dreamer and eagerly recounted his early dreams, which centered on images of his driving the family car too fast and causing damage. This led to discussions of his hidden anger and distaste for authority. He had a great love for sports but longed for something more, and he knew he was underperforming even while getting passing grades. Like his father, he seemed to be settling for less. This extended to both his university career and his personal life. Once he described a dream in which he was arguing with his father about repairs to the deck of the family cottage: his father wanted to repair it piecemeal while Philip opted to tear it up and start over. As we reviewed the dream, Philip acknowledged its implications.

He had been struggling to resolve ambivalent feelings towards his girlfriend. Finally, she called to share her concerns about their future and suggested they separate. Philip was expecting this but still felt a mixture of sadness and guilt. He compared himself to his peers who were seriously dating, thinking that he was failing himself and his girlfriend. As we discussed this, Philip was able to accept the separation. He had been thinking about graduation the next year and moving away from home. I asked him if he was anxious about the possibility of being lonely. He replied that he was comfortable with this and was quite confident in his ability to meet new friends. During this session, he also said that he was seriously considering applying to graduate school. Later on, as graduation approached, Philip decided to take a year off and move back near his home. While there, he felt that he would have the support of his many friends while he pursued his aspirations. One of the most important movements in Philip's therapy was his realization that he could confront his father as well as others in his life – including me.

Irene was a student teacher who came with a history of depression and suicidal ideation. It had gotten to the point that she was scared and had brought herself to a local hospital emergency room. She did not want to hurt her family and felt guilty about having such thoughts.

Irene presented with a bubbly personality and a friendly manner. She had done well in school and was looking forward to graduation, and she approached her student placements with energy and optimism. However, her father had died suddenly six months prior to her seeing me. I felt she was still grieving and placed her on a mild antidepressant. On weekends, Irene would go home to be with her grieving mother and sister, who seemed to be in worse shape than Irene. When she spoke of her father, she glowed with admiration for him. Her pursuit of excellence in her chosen career seemed to be an extension of his goals for her. Despite being quite social with her peers, she felt herself to be alone in life. She would sometimes speak of her dark moments but never elaborate on their content or hold on her. We often had extensive conversations about her teaching and connection with her pupils. With time, her mood improved and she seemed to be moving forward in reconciling her grief. She missed her father, but accepted her new role in life and the pursuit of her career.

I had been seeing Irene for approximately a year when she wrote me an e-mail describing how she had been thinking of killing herself since early adolescence. She was unable to see herself into the future. Irene carried an inner feeling of deadness that belied her outward demeanor. She saw no hope and felt that she was betraying her family's values. One dream seemed particularly poignant. In it, she was standing on the shore of a beach. Out on the lake, she saw her family of mother, father, and sister in a boat. They did not see her and she felt alone. Over time, Irene has been able to express her painful dilemma. Her family has been very good to her but at a great price. Feelings were never discussed directly and secrets forever locked up. Even talking to me raised issues of betrayal of family. Her suicidal gesture elicited more fear than understanding. As a result, Irene believes she was the one keeping her family together at the expense of smothering her most heartfelt desires.

She once recounted a recent family visit. Her mother and younger sister repeatedly argued over the weekend. It reached a point where Irene felt excluded while they continued to argue. She wanted to stop them, tell them how she felt, but remained mute and paralyzed. As Irene told me this story, she was able to summon up her anger. Yet, she had been unable to speak out. That would have been wrong. Her role was to be the peacemaker even at the expense of her own identity.

Most recently, Irene sent me an email as I was about to go on vacation. In it, she recounted the evening before when she struggled with depression throughout the night. Life seemed pointless and suicide a possibility. I tried to reply as best I could but felt rather helpless. I could not find the right words to assuage her despair. She replied that I had not heeded her instruction not to read her note until I returned from my vacation. She then wrote that I shouldn't worry and that it was important for her just to be open with me and share her darkest feelings. The next day she popped into my office looking very bright and almost glowing. She wore a bright shawl and wished me well on my voyage. There was a hint of sexuality, much as a daughter fondly speaks to her father. I felt at that moment we had reached a new level in our relationship.

Yet, we still had to revisit the intense struggle within, the struggle around her true identity. At our next visit, I pushed Irene to come to terms with the distance between her outer sunny face and her inner turmoil. She began to struggle physically, with tears coming down her face, repeatedly saying, "I can't do this." I pushed further, saying, "It's okay to have negative thoughts and feelings." At that point, Irene let out a piercing, shattering scream that bellowed across the clinic and literally shocked me. It was both anger and anguish uttered from the depths of her heart. We sat in silence for a few moments while Irene composed herself and I tried to reassure her that everything was alright. She left a little uncertain that this was true.

However, I didn't call Irene, feeling comfortable with our new relationship.

We met again a week later and reviewed the previous session. She was able to tell me that I was pushing her too hard, but admitted that she realized more clearly the need to get beyond the imprisonment of her early upbringing. We discussed the issue of family secrets and Irene finally grasped how wrong this was. She was able to admit that she had avoided the strong feelings that come with any close relationship, and had begun to realize the need to separate from her childhood.

I could literally feel her emergence and acknowledged the beauty of the moment.

Denise was a twenty-one-year-old student in her second year. She was very engaging and we both shared a passion for sports. For Denise, the guilt surrounding school failure was crushing. Her parents instilled in her the need to graduate and get a good job; however, she just could not bring herself to study and spent most of her time at home staring blankly at her textbooks. As a child, she immersed herself in figurative painting but stopped as an adult. Her father, too, had painted in his youth but abandoned this at university. Denise described him as rigid and very emotional. She felt her mother was intensely focused on success. Denise felt hopeless about her own future with no way out.

Monica was an attractive eighteen-year-old in a science program. She had done well in high school and looked forward to university. She was always very close to her mother who was overprotective; her father was a very successful businessman with many hobbies, but, sadly, he grew distant as she entered adolescence. Monica's mother described him as a brilliant man but rather quiet. As a young child, Monica was rather shy and studious; in adolescence, she became more outgoing and sought attention. At university, she developed multiple physical complaints and became depressed. She began sleeping long hours and failing her courses, her hopes of graduating vanishing daily.

My initial reaction is wonder. These students come from families that were generally supportive, and all had done well in high school. They were able to mask their inner turmoil through scholastic achievement. However, the first year at university presented mounting social and intellectual challenges. Away from parental support, they began to flounder, and this reached a climax in second year. Social withdrawal, depression, and failing grades accompanied a downward spiral. This, in turn, led to inertia and loss of hope.

I approached cautiously, looking for signs of life. I told myself to avoid easy speculation and just to look and listen. I tried to take in the whole person and his or her approach to me. Small gestures and hints of feeling provided early clues – a smile, a sense of humor, a searching look, invited a response. I tried to offer hope and a belief in their future. My approach was to encourage a form of free association. I explained that this was much like the conversations that good friends have with each other. I questioned them about their dreams at our first interview and often offered an initial interpretation of obvious material. The main use of dream reporting is to introduce the student to the realm of imagination, fantasy, and access to an inner life. It affirms this hidden world as a real partner in our endeavour. I encourage my patients to accept their dreams as vital to self–understanding. This prefigures the free associations that will later be the common text of therapy (1).

There were common features that surfaced. All grew up with distant fathers and anxious, loving mothers. Mother also provided a model of endurance and identity. However, I believe the crucial element in each life was the absence of an emotionally present father. Playful encounters were few. Instead they remembered absence, embarrassment, or fear. The sense of play with a father is crucial to self-esteem, sexual identity, and the ability to dream and fantasize (2). An engaged father offers the opportunity to escape the needs of an ever-present mother and embrace an awaiting world. A young person's desires are tempered and shaped by a father's presence in both home and workplace (3). He brings home his daily experiences and fosters adventure. His persistence, despite life's daily challenges, instills courage. His love offers security. The absence of this kind of love delays maturation and undermines confidence. This in turn, reinforces a sense of being different or unworthy. Each disappointment builds on, and magnifies, guilt.

The prospect of university life challenges identity while demanding excellence. Even the social life has a competitive edge. This environment overwhelmed these students. They viewed their problems as a failure to achieve the goals expected by school and family. They were helplessly stuck, with few alternatives. Yet, I felt this was an opportunity for them to dig deeper and to explore themselves. I invited them to speak openly about their hopes and fears, and encouraged them to remember their dreams.

Denise dreamt of meeting a man who might alienate her family. Monica's dreams reflected her struggles to meet the needs of her parents. Philip dreamt he was being chased around a lake by a man with a handgun. He was terrified and hid in a crevice in a nearby hill. He felt safe but strangely suffocated. He was able to associate to the memories of his threatening father and how his own defenses had imprisoned him. (As Philip has matured, his father has mellowed and begun to praise him.) In a vivid dream, Irene saw herself strolling around her university. She wandered into a television room where somebody began chasing her, so she hid behind a couch. This figure was threatening her; then Irene popped up and shot the figure. When she then looked down, she found that she had killed a young girl.

I encouraged these students to examine their history and true identity. They preferred to talk about their failures. I believed this to be a response to early messages to conform and achieve. To live, to acknowledge themselves, stirred memories of ridicule, anger, and fear. I actively confronted their negative thoughts and encouraged dreaming. As our conversations continued, I listened for the subtlest hints of affect. This is where memory hides; it is where the true self lives.

Sara saw herself as someone who was emotionally pushed by boyfriends and family. Instead of confrontation, she preferred silence. Though very bright, she was under-performing and socially embarrassed. Her father was equally shy and reticent. Mother was loving, dominant, and ever-present. Sara's life as a university student opened new vistas, but she was hesitant to be fully engaged. Philip struggled under the shadow of his dominant father. He fully understood his father's limitations, but never rebelled. He hid his strengths and limited his own potential. Throughout her childhood, Denise idolized her father though he became increasingly demanding. As a result, Denise retreated into herself. Monica dreamt of losing a gift given to her by her boyfriend. Each suffered at different times in their lives. Denise was critical of her father but afraid to confront him. Monica could not reach her own potential. Irene's father was a loving presence but emotionally distant. Her admiration of her father prevented her from finding her own identity.

In many ways, each student revived past feelings that sustained their guilt. At each encounter they searched for rejection rather than love. The past hovered over their hopes and desires. They were forced to construct an idealized self they could never inhabit. As their therapist, I sought to eradicate the constricting dictates of the past. But this would come at a significant price, for the loosening of old attachments requires work, commitment, and courage.

The idea of the self is a conceptual framework that describes an individual's search for meaning from the first moments of life (4). Far from being a passive participant, the self actively engages with his or her environment. This occurs well before the development of thought or language. This active engagement is shaped by the responses of the infant's caretakers. They can respond with support or neglect. Sensitive individuals can react badly even to relatively benign frustration. A hostile or inadequate environment can be deadening, resulting in the self's world fracturing and his or her emotions becoming chaotic (5). The true self retreats into the shadows without nourishment and recognition; a false self develops and is mainly defensive and held hostage to the demands of others. Since these earliest experiences occur before the actualization of language, we must glimpse them through their residual affects. I think of the sculptor addressing his task. Through patience and hard work, he chips and chisels away the resistant stone in search of its form. As I approach these young students, I nurture the vision of unlocking this true self.

As therapy unfolded, we confronted rigid ideals embedded in their souls, which had left them captive to parental imperatives. Their individual aspirations were discouraged and there was no room for joy. My aim was to establish a dialogue of self-discovery. And this was not an easy task.

In some ways their failures comprised both pain and comfort. It was a way of being connected to figures they have loved. I tried to establish a dialogue where mutual understanding opens areas of sensitivity and feeling. I offered myself as a collaborator on this journey. Hopefully my associations to their dreams and memories would mirror their private reflections. I understood Sara's need to outgrow her dependency on her mother and encouraged her to embrace her future, so we began to set a date when therapy would end. I reminded Denise of her father's insensitivity to her need to grow. I found myself rooting for her to stand up to him. Monica's father, though brilliant, remained elusive and apart. I affirmed Monica's need for acceptance while praising her individuality. I was excited by Philip's growth and maturation. He was ready to embrace his future, yet still hesitant. When he started dating someone he saw as more experienced, his response was to withdraw and crawl into his inner cave. As we talked, Philip realized that his inner fears deprived him of excitement and joy.

I have struggled to resolve the impasse in their young lives, wondering how I could be useful in their desperation. I sensed their desire for someone to tend their wounds. Am I to be the father they longed for? This seems too easy a solution for me as well as for them. The memories of my father joyfully tossing me in the air fuse with my growing awareness of his immaturity. Yes, their fathers failed them at critical junctures in their lives; but what of the mothers they so fondly remember? Early memories recalled mothers who were depressed and overshadowed by husbands who were distant or critical. These women were unable to provide the strong reassuring presence that soothes a desperately anxious self; therefore, the ability to contain inner fears and emotions was severely compromised. Yet, these students continued to have steadfast attachment to their mothers. The father was just not there as an emotional object. This absence stunted their growth and instilled deep anxiety about reaching out to others and forming lasting relationships (6).

There are hints of deep desires and painful frustration in some of their remarks. Denise often dismissed those who tried to get close to her. Monica would make remarks when I was not attentive enough in a session. I suspect there was much more anger in their hearts than they acknowledged.

As I explored these early memories, the extent of their captivity enveloped our conversations. They had been held prisoner by childhood's frustrated desires. Yet we could face this together with the promise of a better, more realistic, life. I encouraged this movement as each student searched for a new beginning. Sara now sees her future more clearly. She will pursue graduate school and is looking forward to a life away from home. Philip accepts and embraces his potential. He, too, is looking towards an independent future. He is more confident and willing to take risks. Both Sara and Philip have managed to separate from early parental attachment and can look upon their past more objectively.

Irene has embraced her role as teacher and, while struggling with her past, sees her family in a clearer light. Denise had better conversations with her family, resulting in their acknowledging her problems and backing off. They still hoped she would finish school but became more realistic about their goals for her. She, in turn, has made more attempts to complete her courses. I arranged a family meeting with Monica and her parents. They proved to be quite sensitive and supportive and, after some soul searching, Monica decided to leave university and take a year off to find herself. She moved back home, found a job, and registered at the local community college.

I have offered myself to these students as a transitional object and gateway to a better way of thinking about themselves. There is some understanding of this while each remains steadfastly attached to an internally depressed image of themselves. André Green has described this as the "dead mother" at the heart of their darkness (7). Philip and Sara have begun to define themselves. Irene defends her family's values while reaching for her own future. Despite her protests, Denise remains emotionally attached to her parents. Yet the prospect of success and ultimate graduation offers the chance to grow. Monica idolizes and loves her parents while yearning for something more.

I feel the impotence reflected in these young lives and their hesitancy to move forward. I am reminded of Freud's forceful confrontation of such "unwillingness" and his patients' steadfast clinging to old attachments (8). These students have pursued unrealistic goals at the expense of emotional growth. They never learned how to accept the closeness of another. Their isolation was palpable.

Yet, we have reached a point of trust and some measure of mutual collaboration. The next step involves movement towards an interpersonal awareness of themselves and the acceptance of the painful separation from internalized destructive tendencies. My hope is that this time we shared will enable them to take their place in the sun.

References

(1) A Jemstedt and A Phillips, eds. *The Christopher Bollas Reader*. New York: Routledge; 2011, pp. 249-258.

(2) R Mears, *The metaphor of Play*. New York: Routledge; 1993.

(3) C Bollas, *The Forces of Destiny*. Northvale, NJ: Jason Aranson; 1989, pp. 181-199.

(4) A N Shore, *The Science and the Art of Psychotherapy*. New York: WW Norton; 2012, pp.118-143.

(5) G Atwood and R Stolorow, *Structures of Subjectivity: Explorations in Psychoanalytic Phenomenology*. Hillside, NJ: The Analytic Press; 1984, p. 34.

(6) R R Lee and J C Martin, *Psychotherapy After Kohut: A Textbook of Self Psychology*. Hillsdale, NY: The Analytic Press; 1991.

(7) A Green, *On Private Madness*. London: Hogarth Press; 1986, pp. 142-173.

(8) R May, *Love and Will*. New York: WW Norton; 1969, pp. 207-208.

PSYCHIATRIC DISORDERS AMONG SUPPORT PERSONNEL

Captain William F. Kenny, MC*

Description of an Urban Psychiatric Service in Vietnam.

The psychiatric service of the 17th Field Hospital is rather unique among the facilities in Vietnam. The hospital itself is situated in the heart of Saigon and supports some 20,000 service-men as well as all American civilians and foreign nationals work-ing for the U.S. Government. Our in-patient load runs about 20 patients per month averaging three to four days in hospital. This is primarily a transient measure to meet an acute situation. If a patient is seriously ill and psychotic, he is transferred to the 93rd Evac Hospital. The out-patients on the other hand average 110-120 per month. These statistics are composed of roughly 40% evaluation and 60% treatment cases. There are very few psychotics seen on an out-patient basis, the majority being neurotic and personality disorders.

In the Out-patient Department we see almost no cases directly attributed to the strain of combat. By far the precipitating factors are separation from family, marital discord and frustration at work. The presenting symptoms of a mixed anxiety depressive state and those associated with increasing alcoholic intake are particularly common. Another feature of our population is the tendency to respond to stress by misbehaving and incurring some kind of judicial punish-ment. One gains the impression that these people as a whole are singularly vulnerable to loss of external support and through their symptoms attempting to regain that support. As a group they lack strong family ties and are limited in their ability to form solid close relationships. There is usually a history of poor impulse control, lack of judgement and the inclination to rely on others for initiative. On the other hand there is little in the past history indicative of overt psychiatric illness. As an aid to further understanding of the stresses initiating referral, I shall describe some of the more common syndromes seen in the course of the year.

1. Symptoms of Anxiety and Depression.

Many experience initial anxiety with restless sleep and a slight loss of appetite during the first two to three months of their tour. These symptoms are fairly well tolerated and are rarely a cause for psychiatric referral. It is only when this reaction is denied and the conflict somatized that the patient comes to our clinic. Gastrointestinal problems, pain in any area of the body and frequently skin disorders often mask such emotional tension. For the most part these individuals are passive aggressive with little awareness of their own feeling states. Therapy with a mild

*Formerly Chief, Psychiatric Service, 17th Field Hospital, Saigon.

tranquilizer and two to three consultations is usually sufficient to carry them through this period. A more difficult problem is the individual who is experiencing discomfort at being separated from his wife and family. Sometimes this may even be an older person who has managed to have his family with him on prior assignments. Here the symptomatology is quite vague and what comes across is the patient's incessant plea that he cannot stand being away from home. There is a great deal of verbalization of depressed feelings, even crying spells with frequent reiteration of the patient's fears that his marriage is in trouble. Very often too, his wife is a somewhat hysterical type who through her letters indicates that he must find a way to get home. Prior to the referral threats of suicide, AWOL and emotional outbursts have agitated people in the patient's environment to the extent that they too begin to think of ways to get him home. Here the psychiatrist must indicate that what is needed is firmness rather than psychotherapy. Such patients are not ill and once they realize that their immature demands will not be granted, usually make a good adjustment.

2. Alcoholics and Emotionally Unstable Personalities.

This group begins to experience intolerable tension after a few months of initial adjustment. The loss of what little support they had at home appears too much for them. Particularly stressful is the routine of day-to-day life in Vietnam. The emotionally unstable start to complain of boredom, harassment from superiors or experience bouts of affective discharge. It is not an infrequent occurrence in our emergency room for a man to be brought in acutely agitated under the influence of alcohol. Upon waking the next morning there is a period of amnesia for the events that have occurred although the feeling state of being agitated is remembered. There is a serious AWOL threat at this time. In the alcoholic there is a strong feeling of resentment of the government for taking him from a relatively secure environment. He almost expects to be compensated for this "sacrifice" and when he finds himself in a job where some initiative is required he is in trouble. Both of these types of individuals require support and the problem is two-fold: 1) Assuaging the anger of the people in his present environment, 2) helping the man find more a structured assignment. Here ventilation of angry hostile feelings helps quite a bit.

3. Chronic Anxiety States.

Individuals with chronic nervous tension and neurotic anxiety may present at any time during their tour. What seems to happen is that the added stress of adjusting to a new environment makes them vulnerable to the slightest indication that things are not going well. Periodic encouragement and frequent consultations during crises are the rule. Here again physical symptoms may absorb much of the neurotic conflict. Fatigue, tension headaches, insomnia may at first appear to be the initial symptoms of a depression until the marked anxiety becomes manifest. Conversion reactions are rare but the utilization of physical complaints for secondary gain is often employed.

35

19

4. Psychopathic Personalities.

The severe personality disorders as represented by sexual deviates, drug addicts and aggressive personalities are usually referred at a point when they simply want to get out and go home. Unable to completely verbalize their feelings they either allow themselves to be caught or in some way cause enough trouble so as to initiate discharge procedures. Of special interest to me were four men indicted for murder while in Vietnam. In each case the men were impulsive, given to brooding and mildly depressed. The actual killings resulted when the individual could find no outlet for his primitive dependent longings and became enraged. Contrary to the more usual circumstance the victims were not well known or close to the murderer but merely in some way symbolized the frustrating environment.

Perhaps even more significant than the different syndromes is the underlying separation anxiety. During the course of the year I have been impressed with the extent of the dependency needs common to this varied group and the anxiety engendered when such needs are not met. As frustration continues angry feelings arise which cannot be verbalized. The defense mechanisms employed seem primitive: regression to a pleading, dependent state; turning of the feeling against the self inducing an anxious depressed patient; isolation and repression of all affect with resultant boredom; projection of hostile feelings with complaints of harrassment; acting out in a petulent aggressive manner; somatization wherein the patient substitutes one dependent relationship for another. These are attempts to recreate what is felt as lost. With little ability to internalize their previous love objects, support that is not immediately present is not perceived at all.

As a result, there ensues a frantic search for new supporting figures. Very often this is the man's CO or his physician. In these cases, the CO or physician must be helped in dealing with the anxiety such dependency stimulates while the patient has to be taught to verbalize and then tolerate his disappointment and anger.

5. Marriage as a Solution.

Impressed by the extent of the problems engendered by frustrated dependency needs we undertook a study of GIs marrying Vietnamese women. Along with Captain Albert Kastl, Psychologist at the 93rd Evac Hospital we interviewed at random 64 servicemen who were about to marry in Vietnam. In addition, we gave 15 of the subjects an MMPI and selected TAT cards to interpret. An attempt was made to match this group with a control sample of 64 single GIs who were ambulatory non-combat soldiers. In spite of our attempts to match the two groups the marriage subjects formed a distinctly older age range with 75% having over four years service. The soldiers who were marrying gave a history of less sexual activity, a higher percentage growing up in broken homes and 16 out of the 64 having been married once before. Among the control group only three individuals had been divorced and the opinion of these soldiers about American women was much more positive. The general impression gained from this study was that the soldier marrying a Vietnamese girl is somewhat passive and feels threatened by women. This was confirmed by their fantasies of American girls as being dominating, castrating figures. One very significant statistic was the marked paternal death rate among the marriage group lending further support to the thesis that these men lack strong male models to imitate and grew up in a dependent ambivalent relationship with their mothers. The proposed marriage then appeared to be another attempt to solve deep rooted conflicts over dependency needs and in almost all cases was seen as a magical solution for these problems.

No attempt was made to counsel these individuals but the results of the study do offer certain guidelines. On the one hand because of the rather fixed emotional needs of such an individual no amount of direct attempts to discourage him will succeed. However careful eliciting of his ambivalent feelings about women in general and especially his tendency to expect almost no frustration can lead to a more objective discussion of the soldiers' resentment of the American woman. There is in this group a marked tendency to deal with their own angry feelings by projecting them onto women whom they then see as threatening and castrating. As this defense mechanism becomes exposed the individual is faced with the roots of his own hostility and while this may not charge his mind it will at least enable him to see his fiancée in a more mature light.

Summary.

The large majority of referrals to our Out-patient Clinic stem from difficulties centering around unmet dependency needs. The immaturity of these men is quite obvious and more often than not it is the people in their immediate environment who feel pressured into making the referral. A fairly large percentage of this group can be managed in a supportive manner.

Often with the shift towards seeking nurturance from the psychiatrist, the patient makes less demands on the rest of the environment. Some, especially the young adolescents, mature rapidly when presented with a firm but empathic figure with whom they can identify. It is probably the ability to identify with someone in the new environment, be it psychiatrist or CO, or buddy that is responsible for the stabilization of the underlying separation anxiety. Among the more chronic dependent personalities some attempt can be made to neutralize their immature demands. In those instances where marriage is utilized as a magical solution the individual can be helped to a more objective attitude.

In conclusion, it is felt that management of these varied dependency states includes emphasis on verbalization of ambivalent feelings, setting up firm controls, and offering the therapist as an identification figure. With such an approach a large percentage can be maintained in their roles in the community.

37

21

Kenny

Pieces for the Greenwich Time newsletter

by William F. Kenny

Part I Editorials

1983 – 1994

Greenwich Time

BOARD OF CONTRIBUTORS

Peter Abbott
Richard G. Abell
James S. Ardrey
Louis F. Bantle
Edward W. Barrett
Rabbi Richard Block
Charles Bonner
Derek Boothby
Sandra Brant
Peter Briggs
Jerome F. Brodlie
Stephen F. Brophy
Elizabeth Brown
Charles Campbell
Paul Campbell
Janet Caulkins
Frank Coyle
Peter Crumbine
Michael Evan Davis
Tony DiPreta
L. V. Dodge
George Dodson
William F. Douwes
Jerry Dumas
Patrick J. Durkin
Philip Ewald
William Bragg Ewald Jr.

Terence J. Fox
Nancy Godfrey
Pierre Gousseland
William G. Harrington
Lucy H. Hedrick
Paul B. Hicks III
Morton D. Hull
Barbara Hoyt
James Hyde
Pyke Johnson Jr.
Patricia Kane
Karen Kates
John Keenan
William F. Kenny
Al Kestnbaum
Robert G. Lacey
Tim Lanigan
Arlene J. Mark
Bob McGonagle
Kathy McKnight
Jeffrey B. Mead
Shaw Mudge
Joan and John Murphy
The Rev. David Norris
Gunilla Norris
Frank Pace
Norman A. Pederson

Charles Pettengill Jr.
Herman Raucher
Joseph Verner Reed
John Robben
David Ross
William L. Ryan
The Rev. T. Merton Rymph
Phyllis H. Schreiber
Robert Schwartz
James E. Seitz
Albert Sims
Ruth L. Sims
Emerson Stone
Barbara Stretton
Barbara W. Tuchman
Charlee Tufts
Al Varner
Don Walton
Sandra N. Waters
Thomas J. Watson Jr.
John Winthrop
Linda R. Young
Sherry Young
Steve Young
Carole Yudain

Hearst Connecticut Media Group, Norwalk, CT 06851 USA

Greenwich Time, Monday, December 5, 1983 — **A15**

William Kenny

The sharing of experience is the essence of therapy

The image of a child's sandbox has often seemed to me to be the perfect metaphor for therapy. It harkens back to a time when the small child in each of us first learned to play, a time of great promise and great vulnerability.

When I look back to my own first experiences, the fear of strangers and newness mixes with the need for order and mastery, and I imagine a new patient anticipating such feelings. The beginning of therapy brings all kinds of myth and distorted imagery into that first meeting.

The individual in emotional turmoil and pain, seeks relief but only within the context and structure of his or her life's given value system. The patient seeks a solution that will reduce pain, alleviate suffering and make things come out right and invests the therapist with the magic of power and authority.

As we talk, I imagine two children sitting in a sandbox, picking up different toys, warily sizing each other up and murmuring excited cries with each new discovery. Echoes of just such a play experience pervade the first therapeutic hour. Though someone may relate a long and detailed account of his or her life, I think it is rather small gestures towards friendship and intimations of communicability that count the most.

Greenwich Time

BOARD OF CONTRIBUTORS

The sharing of experience is the essence of therapy (continued)

As a means of gaining contact, I believe it important to introduce myself as a person interested in an exchange. While questions help us to catch up to the here and now and provide a general historical account, the idea of a conversation seems more relevant. As matters proceed, my interest naturally focuses on just who this person is and why he is here with me.

An individual's openness toward the possibility of change is critical and must be established early on. Towards this end I try to get beyond the stated reasons for needing therapy and to establish a feeling tone to the meeting that will lift the shadows that darken the memory. This is where the image of two individuals meeting, conversing and getting to know each other is of far more help than the questioning stance of a doctor towards his patient.

The values prevalent in our work-oriented culture offer serious obstacles to the idea of a playful exchange between two adults, especially in such a serious matter. The experience of a timeless contacting and undercurrent of pleasurable sensations inherent in all games seems wasteful and lacks sufficient goals or markers. Yet I believe that the joy of meeting someone new and exciting provides much greater motivation for change than the need to escape pain and boredom.

At first glance, the patient seems intent on recounting instances of failure, hidden fears, and restricting influences. The capacity for joy is often hidden among the details of relationships that reinforce guilt. Very often an individual will indict himself for feeling something when the real problem is that he has not felt enough. The fear of hurting others and the dread of accusations serve to limit vitality and suppress the pleasures of living. It is no small wonder, then, that recurrent depressions occupy a large portion of such an individual's life.

It often seems helpful for me to share something from my own past or inner self. I find that it does not take much to liberate the pent-up energies hidden behind an often bewildering array of symptoms. A smile, a gesture of recognition that far from being a stranger, I am a fellow traveler, recaptures memories long since buried. Everyone has a secret life he longs to share with someone, yet is terribly fearful it is the very thing that will drive people away.

In order to deal with the powerful

defenses against such intimacy, I need to constantly reassure my patient that he or she is in a very safe place. As the fear anxieties subside, I begin to experience the patient in a very different light. Instead of talking at me I now feel the heartbeat of another person and begin to appreciate the power and intensity of this life. As self-confidence builds, new layers are revealed and a personality far more vital emerges.

As therapists we have the choice of either accepting the problems as presented, or looking into the heart of another. This can take many shapes and must be nourished by the sense of mutual recognition and support in the dialogue of therapy. It raises the possibility of great intimacy buffered by the security of a well-defined relationship.

This does not preclude pain and suffering on either side as the prospect of an ending or loss revives the memory of all that we have lost. Childhood rejection can sensitize the soul in such a way that like a frightened and cornered animal, the patient awaits attack and reacts with disguised rage. When this happens, therapy is perceived as a trap or simply not enough to matter. However, by indicating that you do notice and care, hope is kept alive and slowly there is an unfolding as the patient reveals aspects of himself or herself in the manner of a child sharing toys. It is this capacity to enjoy life that somehow must expand, which I as therapist must seek out.

Greenwich Time

BOARD OF CONTRIBUTORS

The sharing of
experience is the
essence of therapy
(continued)

Sometimes a dream or fantasy elaborates the theme of hidden desires threatened by the fear of punishment. This often leads to corresponding memories and fantasies of my own inner world, and helps me to reach an empathic understanding. As the patient gradually begins to see that this type of sharing can be sustained, a definite shift toward mutuality in the relationship occurs and I feel that the individual across from me is actually experiencing me as a person. Sharing, mutuality, feedback, the sense of intimacy, blend progresively and subtlely into a close bond of friendship albeit a special kind.

The knowledge that there must be an ending shapes this friendship and defines the later stages of therapy. The prospect of loss invites all kinds of resurrected pain that the patient has come to accept because, despite the desire to remain dependent, there now a much greater perception of the necessity to move onward.

At this point the idealization of the past begins to fade followed by a deep sense of sadness and mourning. The patient begins to realize that the past was simply not enough and that they indeed want more and can get more out of life. As this process begins to take shape the entire world view changes. Before, everything had been organized to preserve and protect the original experiences of life. As therapy draws to a close, the patient realizes that childhood attachments have kept him or her from a great deal of living.

As patient and therapist reflect on this past, the intimacy of the journey they have traveled dominates the encounter. The future can be embraced because there is an enduring bond that both carry forth within themselves. It a conviction that such a relationship has really counted and meant something of value.

For me, the meaning lies in the power to generate, to succeed in overcoming the deadening influence of the past. For the patient, hope is carried forth in a new belief, a new conception of himself as a person of intrinsic value.

William Kenny, a psychiatrist, is director of the psychiatric clinic at Greenwich Hospital. He is a member of the Greenwich Time Board of Contributors.

William F. Kenny

The diagnosis of madness requires exceptional care

The history of madness contains two contrasting notions. In his dialogues, Plato states that disorders of the soul are primarily disorders of the body. America's first psychiatrist, Benjamin Rush, although he believed lifestyle influenced the degree of insanity, held firm to the idea that a physical disturbance of the brain was its ultimate cause. Even Fraud taught that someday physiology would replace psychology.

The second great notion has its origins among the artists of antiquity who pictured meaning in chaos. The Bible relates how the prophets interpreted dreams and the great romantic writers such as Goethe used metaphorical language to communicate a world beyond logic and rationality.

The madman was accepted as an eccentric but integral part of Western society until the age of rationalism in the 18th century. Then, science and industry left little room for society's rejects, and the mad were locked up along with the poor, the deviant and the criminal. Interestingly, it was as much the protest of his fellow inmates as any enlightened outlook that helped release the mad from such bondage.

Greenwich Time

BOARD OF CONTRIBUTORS

28

The diagnosis of madness
requires exceptional care
(continued)

Modern-day prophets such as Thomas Szasz have raised doubts about exactly who is mad. They attack the medical model and criticize the labeling of individuals as a form of political torture. This is especially true with the diagnosis of schizophrenia. Many believe that within its broad spectrum there are organic as well as psychological conditions. Some see it as a condition of learned behavior in a sick family. Others dare to suggest that psychotic thinking is an adaptive response to a mad world.

There are many individuals whose lives are different. The madman, however, attacks our very understanding of life. Mental functions lose their connection and appear ungrounded. Naked impulses, frightening in their intensity, flare suddenly and language assumes hidden meaning. All sense of time disappears as the past envelopes the present.

In encountering such a person, we are forced back to our own primitive fears and envision a scene in which all control is lost and something terrible happens. Distinctions and boundaries that have helped us survive vibrate with increasing intensity; the lack of such markers assaults our very existence.

This experience with a madman helps clarify our appreciation of a life in which an inner self has never been validated. As a result, he inhabits a world of fragmented perceptions and feelings and cannot identify the ebb and flow of a personal reality. While it is true that all of us struggle with similar conflicts, the madman suffers a primary insult that impairs his meaning. The totality of his being has been affronted; early relationships were never integrated; primitive sense impressions cannot be organized; thinking is autistic; impulses lack structure. Given such a personality, psychotic breakdowns are inevitable, especially when independence and mutuality are expected.

What can we make of this paradox? Is it sufficient to say that people are born this way? Or, as some would have it, that man can be taught madness? We certainly have the impression that such an individual has not learned through others. There is an aura of isolation about the madman that points toward the primitive and original, yet childhood histories are often quite benign. While bizarre mannerisms and excessive preoccupations can provide early warning signals, a mantle of civility often hides an inner reality. Life's milestones come and go with apparent success, but inside nothing has changed. Despite such desolation, there is a will to live, to learn from another. But when all hope is lost, the madman then creates his own caricature of life.

The very young retreat into a game of sound and objects; youths elaborate contrived schemes to block all feeling; adults create their own world, peopled by objects of their imagination and subject to their will.

> Greenwich Time
> BOARD OF CONTRIBUTORS

When we know this history, we realize that the state of madness is a condition of life, not a single event. We are brought back to the beginnings because nothing has really changed since then. The essence of meaning among men has never been felt and explains the strange use of language. The quality of life experienced from the beginning and the availability of warm personal responses to the needs of closeness, love and attention determine not only an individual's feelings toward himself, but also his ability to perceive and move toward the world.

The diagnosis of madness requires exceptional care (continued)

Lacking such support, the madman lives in his inner world with a stubborn insistence, never acknowledging the experience of others. This basic separation from the natural sequence of growth and development forms an enduring liability.

30

The diagnosis of madness requires exceptional care (continued)

The diagnosis of madness requires great care. While disturbances in language and behavior elicit attention and alert our sensitivities, such a profound judgment confronts us personally. As we trace the outlines of a man's past and its connections to his present, we use ourselves as reference points. We search for signs indicating conflict, mutuality and communication. Over an extended period of time we test the capacity to engage in an ongoing relationship.

The sense that a person is truly mad takes hold slowly and is not solely related to differences in thinking, feeling or expression. Rather, it comes from a monumental apprehension of the profound loss of human experience suffered by another. We realize that mutually shared experiences are denied currency in our conversations and that symbols from the past shed no light. Thus crippled, the madman continually exposes his soul.

It is this jagged edge we seek to touch and yet insulate from ourselves. Treatment becomes a reality in which who we are and what we feel are indispensable to another as he begins the slow path towards growth. Such a relationship is as intense and complicated as a mother with infant. It demands total honesty and often seeks total acceptance. Frustration is inevitable along with moments of great pain and joy. The end is uncertain since we are back at the beginning where all things are possible.

―――

William F. Kenny, a psychiatrist, is director of the psychiatric clinic at Greenwich Hospital. He is a member of the Greenwich Time Board of Contributors.

Greenwich Time, Wednesday, April 18, 1984 — **A15**

William F. Kenny
Escaping from loneliness

Alone. It seems I've always remembered being alone. The dark is there like an intimate enemy surrounding me with fear.

At an early age I sought refuge in a fantasy: an Indian princess who could ride a horse, shoot a bow, and was older and distant. I constantly and unavailingly sought her in my dreams. I would call out for her, knowing instinctively that my mother would respond. She would hold me in her lap and rock me into serene and sensual sleep.

I do not know whether I wanted my father to be there as well, but I was aware of his absence, which perhaps kept me feeling alone even while being comforted. Memories of my father give rise to feelings of both affection and anger. He was a man who demanded notice, and he loved to play at life. He was good at games, but if you did not pay attention to him, he would provoke you into some puzzling argument.

Dad could make a simple act of playing catch sheer joy for me, and each time we played he would think up new and more wonderful variations. For a while, I'd feel that I belonged to him, sharing his physical joy. Echoes of his laughter and eccentric humor are timeless rivers in my mind. Yet he was an intensely lonely person, without close friends. He had flourished as the young scion of an Irish tribal family, but never went beyond his upbringing.

Greenwich Time

BOARD OF CONTRIBUTORS

When I was young, he was loving and warm. As I grew, however, he became more distant and more critical. As our relationship grew more strained, I knew that I had to leave home in order to find my own identity. I sought a faraway place insulated from the past — even as his memory tugged at me in various ways. I felt profoundly guilty about leaving this man behind and alone.

Being the oldest, I was always on the verge of discovering family secrets — yet I was fended off. My parents were shy, frightened of themselves, and I learned to leave them be. School beckoned me, and I was determined to make my mark.

I can remember that first day of school. There was a lot of confusion, but I was too afraid to ask questions. The day ended badly with my losing my way, surrounded by children who clearly knew where they were going. Eventually, I reached home, but that part is blocked from memory. I carry with me today that feeling of walking alone, of not belonging, and of being frightened and angry.

Achievement through mastery of language appealed to me powerfully. I read better and faster and loved to stand and recite in class. Although the nuns were grim and forbidding, performing for them gave me status and confidence. One particular nun, however, was younger and fairer than all the rest. She was my Indian princess incarnate, and I her favorite student in the second grade. Her interest had an aura of warmth that

Escaping from loneliness
(continued)

still lingers in my memory.

I had always been interested in philosophy and the mystery of life, probably as a means to examine my own life. Medicine was a compromise, a way of being priestlike in a profession. It seemed to offer rational answers. Yet its density frustrated me, and medical school and internship became repetitive work, unexciting and isolating.

As a young physician, I was constantly aware of my limitations, and certainly did not see myself as a healer. Several events subsequently changed the interior of my life. I met an outgoing fellow resident in psychiatry. He taught me the value of people and the need to care.

My year in Vietnam as a field-hospital psychiatrist underlined the need to survive through depending on others. Returning to America, I found a love that was simple, beautiful and freeing. These were steppingstones that gave me the courage to enter analysis. The final decision, however, was prompted by considerble personal anxiety, reflecting a turning point in my life.

Greenwich Time

BOARD OF CONTRIBUTORS

My analyst was brilliant and somewhat aloof. I am still indebted to him because more than anyone he liberated the power within me. At first we sat and talked together face to face. Later, when he felt I could tolerate the intimacy, I lay down on the couch and began my analysis.

I found it difficult to let go of my defenses. His presence, always insisting I could go on, forced me into awareness of interior recesses that were both exciting and frightening. Dreams ushered in eerie conflicts from years past, but the act of relating such fantasies to another stripped them of their ethereal quality, and helped me to reclaim as my own what I'd long ago disowned as shameful and embarrassing. I can see now that I started growing, healing, when I began to experience myself as a bodily presence. I became more assertive, more encompassing.

Yet it was the memory of my childhood that stirred my soul. I discovered that the irrational inner world of imagery that inhabited my past was the power I needed to continue the search for that long-sought princess. Far from being demonic, I discovered that this inner world reached out to embrace my fellow man. I also came to know that what we all tend to hide is often the best that is in us.

It has become the germ of an idea that therapy, directed at this source of creativity, can liberate untold energy. I would seek, then, the private world of others, not as a judge, nor even as an educator, but rather as a fellow participant.

William F. Kenny, a psychiatrist, is director of the psychiatric clinic at Greenwich Hospital. He is a member of the Greenwich Time Board of Contributors.

William F. Kenny

Journeying back in memory to a place called adolescence

I try not to go back to that time of pain and self-consciousness. Yet I must, since two boys, 13 and 11 years old, depend of my ability to remember and to relive it in a better way.

Theirs is the face of youth: alive to new possibilities while secure in the love always awaiting them. The frightening void that can only be filled by their willingness to act, to create themselves as unique stars on the horizon, moves closer in time and threatens to engulf us. Looking at them, those two boys, experiencing their laughter, feeling their trust, returning now the look in their eyes brings me full circle to my own youth and that age of desire.

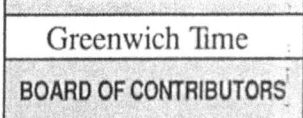

Greenwich Time
BOARD OF CONTRIBUTORS

It was a period of desperately wanting to be me and not knowing how. The wanting to be one with others was hidden behind a screen of shyness. I would look at someone only to turn away from a smile. I remember the waiting most of all. My friend and I haunted the corners of our world looking and waiting for someone to arrive and something to happen. Time would not be a friend in those days as we awaited our cues. I hear those two boys of mine today and sense their need to possess themselves, their bodies, their future. I want them to be actors, out front singing their song. I know it will be painful for them as it was for me.

34

Journeying back in memory
to a place called
adolescence (continued)

We live in a world buffeted by the winds of change, where growing up lacks safe harbors. Sometimes when I catch them watching me, I dream of forever. The warmth of their accepting hands seems enough to still time and keep the angels in the sky. Then, subtle warning signals reflect the coming storm and a frown steals across brows of innocence. Childhood has come and gone and with its passing we have all lost the comfort of a friend.

I wonder how we shall embrace the future and honor the past when our culture demands only a present. The uncertainty of the task ahead has been affirmed by the anguished testimony of a violent decade. Dying and the romance of death have spread like a prairie fire among the hearts of our youth as they despair of self-discovery. The passage rites, the bravado, the coupling and banding together serve as distractions from the secrets within. We are all perhaps too busy to hear their struggle, too eager to suspend their play, too serious to tolerate their feelings.

Greenwich Time
BOARD OF CONTRIBUTORS

Adolescence is a long goodbye filled with memories, surrounded by hope. It is too crowded and demands resting places. During these times, I can share with two boys our common history and enjoy the timeless feeling of together. Such moments can only be brief: I sense their need to move on. Once again, I feel the old conflicts and catch myself responding too quickly, as if it were still my battle and not theirs.

I can see myself again looking to possess the future and spin my desires into a many-colored garment, rich with the joy of life. Now they need to test the ground, each in his own way shaping a destiny that will inevitably sever the past. I find that I must trust in them more than I could ever grant myself. At those times when there will be clashes of wills, I can only hope that I have the strength to say: "Be true to yourselves, not me. Create your own story. Go — run with the wind."

William F. Kenny, a psychiatrist, is director of the psychiatric clinic at Greenwich Hospital. He is a member of the Greenwich Time Board of Contributors.

35

Dreams reflect our deepest, sometimes lost, lives

By William F. Kenny

Near and
Hard to grasp is the god
But where danger is
The deliverer too grows strong

In the darkness dwell the eagles
But fearless man remains as he
must
Alone before God; simplicity protects
him
And no weapon needs he and no
Cunning till the time
When God's failure helps
— Hoderlin

Our dreams speak to us in fragments revealing the underside of our lives. The people of antiquity were much closer to nature than we are today and took seriously this other-worldly experience. Whether interpreted as a magical omen or a message from God, the dream held a respectable place in their culture. As formal religions and then science succeeded in categorizing our experiences, the dream lost its significance as a guiding spirit.

Freud declared the dream to be the "royal road to the unconscious," indicating its importance to any understanding of self. The evidence is quite clear that we dream every night and that this activity is necessary to healthy adaptation to life. When individuals are prevented from dreaming in the sleep laboratory, the sleeper compensates by increased dreaming on subsequent nights. Yet many people do not remember dreaming or find the experience lost like quick-silver upon awakening.

Such difficulty in recovering dreamlife often disappears as patient and therapist jointly explore their myriad perceptions, feelings and responses during the therapy hour. As trust develops and mutuality deepens through a shared vulnerability, I find that another's images and dreams play upon deeper chords in *my* being. Memories of my own magical history float like tiny capsules of time across my brow:

I enter sleep uneasily, passing into another dimension. There are no easy landmarks and everything seems odd and uncertain. Time races ahead, bringing people and places in and out of focus. Events from the past reach out and draw me back to a land of conflict and desire.

I see a young boy, kneeling, and above him the face of a woman. In the silence, I look for my mother, but she is not there. Yet my brother, whom I fought often, appears close by, revealing a tenderness never shown in childhood. A buried moment summons darker rhythms as shadows leap from walls to reflect the cries of passions come and gone.

Dreams have run like a river through my soul: I remember the figure of a man dressed in black staring at me unsmilingly. I try to avoid him but am drawn forward in strange fascination. I come near only to awaken to the sounds of the street outside my window. The laziness of the city noises contrasts strongly with the quickened activity of my imagination. Compelled by the reality of the hour and the night, I lose the meaning of this strange journey.

There is a sense of childlike wonder in our dreams that captures the self constantly searching. In the daily conversation of our lives, we manage to project society's need for order and direction. However, when the dreamworld unveils its hoary demons, I no longer can be so certain.

I am surprised and sometimes embarrassed by the self I see. Feelings and impulses that by day seem trivial often become bizarre figures in a visual parade: A flash of anger hurls spearlike toward scampering bodies as storm clouds shape a threatening horizon. Rushing about for shelter, I am ushered into a many-roomed house by gentle hands. I hear again the laughter of voices and feel the familiar intimations of childhood.

There within the warm glow of security I rest for awhile. Old wounds heal, nursed in the arms of caring friendship. A wisp of hair made golden by a single shaft of light circles just beyond touching. A sudden change shifts the scene as if in a movie. Someone, vague and sexless, calls out the names of pris-

oners, and once bright windows become dim and far away.

A crowd of faces runs down an endless corridor, forcing a glance backwards into yet another memory: A small child conjures images from soft moonlight while echoes play among gravestones late on a Sunday afternoon. I catch myself swimming alone in a quiet ocean, sensing the deep.

Our dreams speak to us in fragments revealing different selves. The ancients saw in them God's spirit, and today's therapist listens to the dreamer for clues to his personality. Yet this view of the dream as hidden and alien misses its dynamic force. In order to accept such a unique experience, we must separate from a world that celebrates reason over emotion. Today, it seems that only children and artists are allowed such freedom. Perhaps that is why the patient in childlike trust can once again share with me his vulnerability.

This gift plays upon the deeper chords of my being and releases images bound by sanctions frozen in everyday language: Near an aging forest, there is a verdant field undulating beneath a sun that never sets. Far off in a corner of this vision, a man emerges from the round lip of a dark tunnel. He blinks his eyes unused to such bright light and slowly, unsteadily raises himself to his full height.

The look on his face describes pain and determination mixed with sadness. It is obvious that he is glad to be in this field but has left something or someone dear to him behind. As he walks forward his gait falters as if caught or tugged at, but he moves on intently and with more forceful stride. The beauty of the day and the hills and the field is overwhelmingly joyful. He cocks an ear expectantly, for the land invites the feeling of life. Yet there is no sound. He is alone and frightened but walks on singing to himself as God whispers through the trees.

Yes, we are a race of dreamers painting messages wherever we go.

William F. Kenny, a psychiatrist, is director of the psychiatric clinic at Greenwich Hospital.

Greenwich Time, Wednesday, December 18, 1985 — **A15**

The Rev. O'Connor's belief in humanity

By William F. Kenny

I grieve for him even now, this man of God. He managed to fool us into believing him holy when in fact he was merely doing his job. He rests in the stillness of his church while looking out from a carefully wreathed photograph. Hands are folded and dark eyes stare serenely over a pleasant smile. This picture, though, gives little of the man and seems more sculptured than real. There is nothing of the inner tension clawing at the edges of his skin. His walk suggested struggle and intensity and yet as one drew closer, a gentle warmth reached out in greeting. I would see him on his way to the hospital or more usually catch his bent figure peering over name cards at the admissions desk, a fisherman preparing his net. We'd stop and chat for a minute and he'd go on his way, alone it seemed yet with a purpose, for he was there to be with someone, to share another's pain. He puzzled me in the way that truth grabs us and refuses to let go. He had the air of an ascetic and at first appeared a fragile, shy man. I think now that he used these qualities to disarm, for he was also a man of tremendous power. He made you feel important because he listened and cared. This was his secret, caring about and for individuals. And he understood clearly the need for strength in dealing with the evils in our society.

Because of his convictions and because he was Irish I think, he became a master at forging alliances, a builder of bridges between men of differing beliefs. His church and his people scattered far and wide in deed and word to bring consolation and hope. At the same time he fought strenuously to give his own priests the freedom to think and to speak out. His home at St. Catherine's was a place to come and stop for awhile and to grow.

I wondered at his optimism in the face of adversity. Tomorrow invariably brought solutions because he worked very hard to bring them about. Believing in God, he did not leave much room for chance. His was a faith deeply rooted in the human endeavor and listening to him talk about future projects. One could feel him contacting his God in daily ministry. Above all, he was a pastor spending his energies tending to business. In a modern world and church he held on to habits chiseled from a lifetime of inner direction. He could be stubborn and sometimes was wrong. He died rich in a sea of affection carrying our burdens. I shall miss him and his sense of mission. His presence stirred belief, his absence is hard to comprehend.

There is a strong irony in the way this priest and man died. He was given a jubilee crown and was at the height of his powers when the blow came. New directions were promising greater opportunity and he was looking forward to an even richer ministry. A jealous God, it seemed, snatched him away from us. It must have been the hardest thing of all to accept for this man of driving compassion. Like Christ, like Augustin, his mission was not complete and there was much work to be done. His words to us contained, however, only a hint of that inner stuggle and in the end he accepted all. He gave himself back to us in care and concern, sharing his deep faith in a loving God. For a man who cared so much for his people, saying goodbye must have been an agonizing moment. Through such faith and unyielding spirit he is once more among us. I hear him walking the halls of the hospital and see his presence in his church, his parish, his town. His steps are lighter now and his eyes carry less struggle. He is with his God and has reached into all our hearts.

William F. Kenny, a psychiatrist, is director of the psychiatric clinic at Greenwich Hospital.

A desperate loneliness and the rage of angels

By William F. Kenny

I see them in the morning, standing alone or in small groups. Each is a small universe staring at the coming day. They shuffle together, occasionally speak but rarely smile, as if protecting some secret. The school bus arrives and they disappear into a world I have long forgotten.

As I pass by, I feel their vulnerability and wonder how much time is left before we envelop their souls with our desires for mastery and power. They are so young, so full of hope for a future they cannot possess. We offer them the illusion of wealth and the need for success. In such a world, only the strong, the quick and wise have market value. We will have no truck with Milton's "They also serve who only stand and wait."

A face bearded with anxiety looks into me questioningly: "Will I be all right? I'm worried what to do next. I have no place to go." What do I say to this gentle man filled with a rage he cannot know. He drinks to the point of oblivion so that he can go on. Some years past he, too, took a school bus filled with dreams. And he almost made it to the top, vice president of an investment company. He believed in the American myth of winning and in the process denied his strong needs for love and caring. Now all he has left are those needs and no place to rest his head. Another, a woman, calls out in anger. "Why must it be me? Whenever I call out for help, no one is there." We have gone over this refrain many times and I have tried to help her see how she creates her own isolation.

Greenwich Time

BOARD OF CONTRIBUTORS

'The heart of such barren landscapes is the emptiness of family life and the lack of any form of intimacy.'

May 2, 1986

Underneath her need and her anger, however, is an even deeper anguish. She is afraid of her own loving, as if to feel for someone is to destroy him or her. As a young child she was bright and beautiful. She was led to believe that being best was all that mattered and so took on roles, performed instead of growing. Even as a patient, there is an acted-out quality to her which limits feeling and true awareness.

A desperate loneliness
and the rage of angels
(continued)

Recently I was asked to interview a young boy hospitalized because of his frightening anger and abuse of alcohol and drugs. In the course of our conversation it became apparent that he was quite depressed at the loss of a relationship with a girl much younger than himself. The adults in his life thought this an unnatural friendship and quickly ended it.

He sits now in a hospital cell, uncommunicative, angry, without hope. I want to shout: "Stay with it, your time will come. Above all, keep hoping." And, in truth, for most this rings true. But some are scared in a way that sees even a helping hand as a veiled attack. One of my patients recently hurled his rage at me for trifling with his mind, for intruding into his inner world. I was taken aback, frightened for the moment and yet keenly aware of a pain so deep his ability to trust is seriously impaired. As a result he withdraws behind a wall of symptoms, a mystery even unto himself. New relationships are approached without the thrill of discovery and merely used to dredge up his past.

The heart of such barren landscapes is the emptiness of family life and the lack of any form of intimacy. People exist in the same house but rarely speak to each other. There are so many other claims to one's attention. The world beckons with its promise of a life rich with pleasure and success. It is no wonder that people start to play roles in order to please others, to accommodate to their expectations. In the process, identity is lost and the soul exists in a borderland of doubt and lost opportunities. The real pain of growing and the joy of sharing is never talked about and never sought.

Everyday the headlines in our papers portray the urgent cries of our young people. Drugs, suicide, vandalism and violence, what are these but the drifting cries of vulnerability in a noisy and narcissistic society? We must return to a time of simplicity. The structure of family life with its inner force and harmonious communication needs resurrection and focus. When I think of family, I think of a place in which to sit and to be. It exists nowhere and yet everywhere and stands outside of time. Within its borders truth is supreme and each is free to love one another. Our modern society distrusts this inner world, laying siege to it daily.

When I meet with couples who have come apart, the most common problem is an inability to carve out time to be with each other. It seems that the simplest of elements, time, has been fragmented and parceled out to a variety of impersonal agendas. It is strange that the desire for oneness is so easily distracted by false Gods. As we talk, I often ask them to trace the hopes each partner brings to the other. In so doing, the shadows of life's earliest moments penetrate and surround our conversation.

Accusation and resentment give way to a deeper vision, and childhood's time is rekindled in the ashes of lost opportunities. As each person is encouraged to share their needs, the fear of rejection pales and loving is risked again. This I truly believe is the essence of the healing experience: to be able to be who we are in the presence of another. Without it we can only hear the silence of God and the rage of angels.

William F. Kenny, a psychiatrist, is director of the psychiatric clinic at Greenwich Hospital.

Greenwich Time, Wednesday, May 21, 1986 — **A15**

Spirit of the soul can overcome physical suffering

By William F. Kenny

There is a serious question hovering over the bodies of our sick and disabled. In a land dominated by industrial might, a high crime rate, daily violence and adolescent suicide, we debate the right to die. It is ironic that we question the meaning of dying, at a time when the issue of values in our daily life has all but disappeared. Death had always seemed the one mystery we dare not explore, God's last domain. The religionists insisted on the importance of the soul, not the body. As a result, we reverently withdrew from those last private moments. We held as cherished beliefs the notion that God chose the hour and the day, according to His plan and His purpose.

Now the focus has shifted. God is out of the picture altogether, and the soul is rarely mentioned. Rather, it is man's body with all its wondrous mechanisms that is now on display. Medical science has pushed life's frontiers further than anyone had ever dreamed. We travel from birth to senescence with great alacrity and must confront the manner in which death takes place.

The living will has become the symbol of our concern. We will control our destiny right to the end. There is no passive acceptance in this imagery. The last rites seem irrelevant when one has already made such a disposition. The issue turns on the question, "Whose life is it anyway?" posed by the Broadway play a few years ago. In this secular age whose boundaries are uniquely self-centered, we have become increasingly convinced of the

Greenwich Time

BOARD OF CONTRIBUTORS

right over our own bodies. We abort, we declare war, we commit suicide. Why, then, should anyone question the right to die? It is assumed as part of the air we breathe.

Any consideration of death must start with the examination of the need for meaning in our lives. As we grow into adults, this quest becomes an intense hunger, never quite fulfilled. Life offers glimpses of something beyond ourselves, yet remains essentially impenetrable. Hence, the projection of a future bright with possibilities. Yet, the closer we get to catching hold of our own identity, the more limited questions we ask of ourselves. It is almost true that in order to fully live in the present, we must give up something of our future. Death and the prospect of dying is the ultimate boundary.

Since all must face this reality, it bestows a kinship upon those who touch its shadows. It is the time when meaning in our life demands definition. With the advent of our technical ability to prolong even terminal illness, such a time takes greater shape as a specific period with appropriate tasks. There is the need to take stock of all that we have been and to confront our failures. It is a time to say goodbye in ways that underscore the values

Spirit of the soul can
overcome physical suffering
(continued)

inherent in human relationships. Family, friends and caregivers need to have the courage to share this pain and yet communicate their own vitality.

Too often the terminally ill are prematurely buried by the flight of the living. For these reasons I have frequently encouraged the acknowledgement of anger in the encounter with the dying person. Real feelings support the hope in each of us that we have finally mattered. In this process, old wounds find healing and family dynamics are formulated with a meaning and richness newly discovered.

In our busy hospitals, the professionals have become absorbed with technical advances at the expense of humanity. The task of sharing these very personal burdens is left to others. One such group of volunteer women at my own hospital, spend their time getting to know and to befriend the terminally ill. They tell of the honesty, courage and anguish it has been their privilege to share with very unique individuals. They truly live this time with the dying and acutely feel the loss. In doing this work, they help to affirm personal value. Such an understanding has led to the development of the hospice movement in our own and other hospitals across the country.

If dying then is a normal phase of life, why do we repress it's meaning? Pain, suffering and loss of function challenge and frighten us, but should not lead to despair. There can be meaning and hope and much living when those involved truly give to each other. I take issue, then, with those who want the end to come quickly, to be snuffed out like a candle at a birthday party.

Very often the source of despair in seriously ill persons is not the prospect of dying, but rather the isolation it entails. No one really wants to talk to them, and yet the time is short and there is a lot to say. It is not a time to play roles, and yet the dying are often trapped by the inability of the living to communicate with them. This is especially true in families who have practiced avoidance over the years. In one sense, this represents their last chance to be real. Of course, our mind shudders at the prospect of our bodies riddled with pain and a useless burden to others.

It makes no sense to continue when considered from this view. However I hope that the decisions made reflect a recognition of the spirit inherent in all of us. I am an individual person with a specific history and a given set of relationships. This event we call death is a mystery in search of meaning. Such a meaning finds its resolution in quiet moments of silence which shatter illusion. In our rush to end anxiety and find easy solutions we have narrowed our focus and stilled the voice of the spirit. I hope that as we debate the right to die, we keep in mind the obligation to live, to be rather than not to be. When we speak of the death of a man, it is always a matter of the soul, never the body.

William F. Kenny, a psychiatrist, is director of the psychiatric clinic at Greenwich Hospital.

• Greenwich Time, Wednesday, January 7, 1987

Practice of medicine must reclaim its human face

By William F. Kenny

I had come with trepidation. McGill University was some distance and I had not seen but one or two fellow students in 25 years. I remembered those four years in medical school and the difficulties of its painful realization. My own ambivalence, then as now, cast a shadow on the tasks before me. Yet, here I was, returning, seeking to touch something elusive in that beginning of my career as a physician and healer.

The first night, with its pervasive warmth and fellowship, awakened strong feelings of brotherhood as I met those faces from the past. We relived the years and brought them forward, hungrily catching up on each classmate's current endeavor. The memories rushed at us like a strong tide carrying in its wake the bonds of a commitment forged with hope. We had wanted to accomplish something, to matter, and to conquer sickness. The next day, in a more formal way, we shared those 25 years in a parade of heroes.

One by one, my comrades spoke: They were clinicians and research scientists, as well as administrators and family practitioners. Each brought his or her personal perspective on a quarter century of high ideals and earnest purpose. What a wondrous sight it was, to see and hear men and women still fresh in their desire to heal the sick and comfort the weak.

As I listened, I felt excited. I was part of something much larger than myself, realizing at that moment the heroic tradition we singly and collectively shared. All the pain and effort of those years came to a single focus in the conquest of knowledge over disease. We had ridden the rising crest of medicine and helped transform dreams into reality. We had pushed back the threat of illness and rescued our neighbors both in peace and war. There was, and still is, something romantic in the calling of medicine, something despite its burdens, that has kept us young at heart. I watched the faces in the room and saw life's meaning reflected in eyes still bright. No, the flame had not died with the passing of years; I knew and felt great pride in being a member of a truly noble profession.

Returning home, I have found the excitement of renewal blunted by present reality. Our great hopes have fallen victim to an insidious predator. Corporate America has discovered the business of medicine and is gnawing at its entrails. Managed health care is, I fear, here to stay. Hospitals are beginning to lose their identity, as large medical empires emerge. The individual physician is

Practice of medicine must
reclaim its human face
(continued)

'The industrialization of medicine has reduced our behavior to a frantic battle for survival, while businessmen peer over profit and loss columns.'

slowly being replaced by impersonal groups and medical organizations. This industrialization of medicine has reduced our behavior to a frantic battle for survival, while boardrooms of businessmen peer over profit and loss columns. The buzz words of the corporation, cost efficiency and quality control, have invaded the hospital corridors.

Outside, old people die and the poor roam the streets, homeless and confused. Our institutions have found the simplest route to efficiency and survival: eliminate the problems by not letting them in the door. The hospital, once a sanctuary for the poor and the crippled, has lost its meaning amid the cash-flow zealots of a sanitized society.

It is true that we have much to regret. We forgot our place as servants and started to believe that society owed us a rich living. In the rush to success, many of us simply became too busy to practice good medicine. Finally, we convinced ourselves that healing was a scientific and technical process, thereby eroding the personal, intimate art of the healer. We are now paying for these sins as Mammon devours the legacy of our noble predecessors. Yet, I cannot help but believe that we still have much to offer our fellow man. Most of us share a singular desire to care for the sick and to fight illness. There is still a bit of the romantic in us, keeping alive the desire to do the very best we can. We still challenge death each day and carry home the pains of this struggle. We are witnesses to affliction and have not abandoned our quest.

The next decade will be a watershed for American medicine. At its end we either will have survived, or we will slowly deteriorate in a series of violent death rattles. The outcome is in the balance, as the impersonal forces of our society envelop the individual and embattled physician. While still occupying an esteemed position, today's doctor

Practice of medicine must
reclaim its human face
(continued)

faces gradual erosion of his identity and professionalism. Sadly, he has been forced to exchange the traditional role of physician-healer for that of scientist-businessman. The art of medicine requires a large dimension of time and leisure. You cannot hurry a sick mind or wounded body without interfering with nature's need for a healing experience. Patients need such time to unravel from their daily cares and anxieties. The doctor needs time to focus on the deeper realities of the person in his office.

One of our greatest physicians, William Osler, taught that the essential ingredient for diagnosis and cure was empathic listening. Our economic-oriented marketplace abhors such time consuming inefficiency. We prefer science to art.

As a result, we are relegating the healing function to the margins of our society. It is ironic that our modern technical hospitals spawn distrust and malaise, while practitioners of various stripe lure our patients outside its walls. Yet these shamans speak to a voice in all of us that cries out for understanding. The diseases of men and women need to be perceived and experienced as personal encounters, not mechanical failures. The suffering and pain in another's eyes must be engaged if hope is to prevail.

The physician of old faced illness with little but his spirit to encourage his patient's will to survive. He often experienced failure, but, surprisingly, he witnessed man's triumph as well. It was a shared encounter in which the healer took on the pain and anguish of the suffering patient. In a way, he accepted illness to know it better and to conquer it in a very personal way.

This sense of sharing between patient and doctor has been lost in the victories of modern medicine. Our technical skills and ability to conquer certain diseases have expanded exponentially. However, newer illnesses arise from the ashes of our cures and our patients, our neighbors, feel alienated and angry at us.

Did we promise too much and fail? Or is it nature's way of humbling all who ignore her rhythms and mystery? In a land made arid by big government and big business, the reality of anguish and the whispers of the dying beckon us to come closer. Standing there, waiting for the end we must all endure, we will perhaps hear again the call to greatness.

William F. Kenny, a psychiatrist, is director of the psychiatric clinic at Greenwich Hospital.

45

An uneasy struggle through therapy

By William F. Kenny

She sits across from me inflamed with rage. This woman of talent and intellect cannot find her soul. The image of a sad burdened face beckons from childhood. The power of that moment embraces her entire world, casting a bitter irony onto each relationship.

I return her defiant stare, uneasy in my attempt to define myself as a sympathetic listener. I have offered to try to help this woman find meaning in her intensely personal struggle. Yet I know she views me with distrust. In her need for me, my patient must defend against the power I have to enter the interior recesses of her memory. In so doing, I resurrect echoes of a hated past and cause her to feel the helplessness of someone unable to speak to the one she loves most in the world. Although I offer my friendship, she is bound to see me as an enemy.

Listening to her tale of deprivation draws me into an inevitable paradox. This unloved and unloving woman demands an unequivocal, all-encompassing love be given her as just due.

What was once lost in time must be retrieved at the expense of others. For her, I am not merely here to facilitate understanding and growth. Rather, she sees me as the embodiment of all that she must have to feel alive. As our dialog intensifies and her hunger deepens, the fear that she will lose again becomes overwhelming. At this point she is forced to attack me as unreal and trivial while clinging to a lost paradise. I can hear the echoes of her earliest struggles. Her alienness strikes a particularly vibrant chord in me. I would like to call her mad and leave it at that. Yet, the sorrow in her anguish is compelling and we continue.

Our patients often come to us in acute despair or unsettling anxiety. The security of their world has been threatened by loss or change, raising again the question of enduring trust. For some, adaptation makes impossible demands. There is no coherent sense of self, no reservoir of positive feeling to draw upon. The heart of their experiences is empty and blank, and the life they lead is a parasitic attempt to feed off the energies of others. And always there is the terror of being exposed.

Greenwich Time
BOARD OF CONTRIBUTORS

The only defense against possible annihilation becomes the manipulation of events and people. They move through life carefully measuring the emotional space in their environ. This chameleon existence cannot feed the inner desire for completion and gives birth to the fantasy of magical union with an all-giving companion. The desire for such a redemptive love can often lead to the denial of reality. Once attached to someone, that person is seen as the source and ground for almost everything. All the while, the dread of exposure lies hidden beneath this brittle veneer. Not many relationships can survive such a shaky underpinning and soon the unreality produces uneasiness and withdrawal on the part of the love object. The only recourse then is unspeakable rage at the now-threatening love object, who is perceived as heartless and deceptive.

The beginning of therapy often promises more than is delivered. This is especially true when encountering someone whose life seems without self respect. While listening, I can only hear the cry of anguish and the rage of defeat. My patient accuses me of offering triviality. In such a wasteland, what succor can words provide? My first task is to survive what no one else has endured. This involves the acceptance of my own limitations and the unhappy knowledge that there are many I cannot help. Yet I am here in this place at this time to listen and respond. The echoes of my own childhood intermingle with my patient's drama. I hesitate to turn back to the beginnings of such emptiness. In so doing, I seem at times trivial even to myself.

All movement ceases as she guards access to the past with the ferociousness of a lioness. Yet, I see that little girl, burning with a tremendous love in a darkened room. She calls out in need and desire, desperate for a response. No wonder my silence impales her during our time together. She repeats to me a litany of defeat, almost exulting in the ability to negate. I can hear the child again looking softly for some hint of applause.

There is a center in each of our lives that gives value and meaning. For her the past is always present, while for me, the present shapes a future I cannot see. Somehow the two of us must accommodate our differences and come to a meeting ground. Our common enemy shares the shadowy space between us like a black widow spider ready to devour her mate. My approach is cautious so as not to disturb the anxious moment in our hearts. I recognize the delicate predicament I must present — any movement creates danger. A new and different web spun from the rhythm of mutual need may offer temporary sanctuary. In answer to her fear, I suppress the instinct to turn away. Out of the shadows a young child screams in the night. It is not terror, but rage at an indifferent world, hurled across the years.

The right to need another is a hidden virtue in our society of achievement. We cast it away to secure the praises of those bereft of their own identity. Like lemmings, we race to our destruction blindly driven by the promises of a vanishing tomorrow. In the silence of therapy, however, a glance carries great weight. At those times when I am too occupied to notice, the old distrust returns with vehemence.

Sometimes I am caught off guard when a patient tells me I should have been more sensitive and listened to what he or she intended, rather than the words occupying our space. Slowly, however, we come to a compromise where I am willing to be taught and my patient accepts the hiddenness of my own desire. We begin to create a special intimacy built around the mutuality of work. Our task is to build a future that will survive the end we commonly grieve. Towards that end, we dedicate ourselves to a noble vision, that of artists preserving value beyond the noisy insensitivity of those we love. Having killed the demons gnawing at our hearts, we must move onwards.

William F. Kenny, a psychiatrist, is director of the psychiatric clinic at Greenwich Hospital.

46

Adult life, childhood fears

By William F. Kenny

There was, not far from our house in Brooklyn, a small park. It had gently rolling hills, a playground, and lots of green grass. However, I was seldom allowed to go there because my mother felt it was unsafe. The idea that something awful might happen to me just a few blocks from home defined the limits of my adventures as a young boy. It cast an envelope of fear around the spirit of my imagination. Whenever I return to that old neighborhood, I am impressed by the innocence of that park and the anxiety it generated in my parents.

Greenwich Time

BOARD OF CONTRIBUTORS

When confronted by new and frightening experiences, we tend to return to what is familiar and safe. Sometimes this turning backwards acts only as a defensive flight and we fail to adapt and grow. Detailed observations of young children demonstrate repeatedly the importance of a mother's supportive presence for a child to explore his or her surroundings. From such early beginnings, we develop self-confidence and a zest for life. For some, however, the earliest beginnings are veiled in darkness. As a result, security needs underlie all of their actions. While this limits much of their potential, it is even more destructive in intimate relationships. When we meet someone so impaired, our own enthusiasm for life feels constricted. This is equally true in therapy, where the battle to contact the past is often blocked by a memory darkened with fear and pain. The ensuing struggle becomes an intense effort to revive the passion for adventure, to encourage the risks of living.

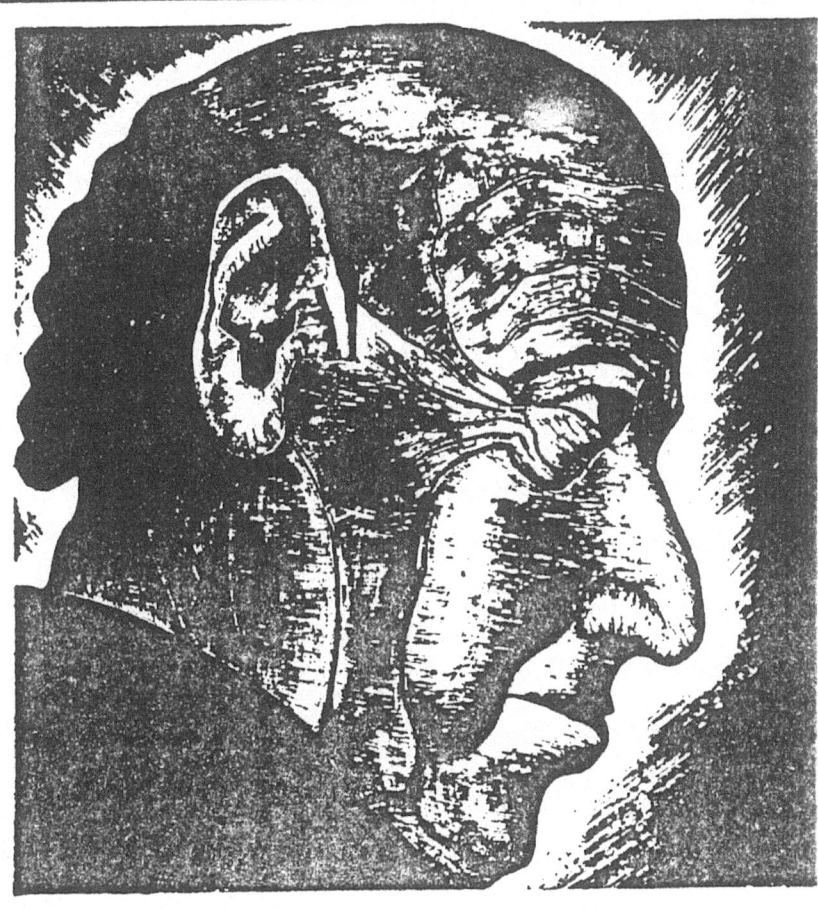

The memories of childhood permeate our lives in many subtle ways. When I think back to that time of fragile identity, I remember feeling anger at the insensitivity of those around me. However, I never really expressed my discomfort, cowed perhaps by my parents' exuberance and eccentricity. As a result, these memories remain as disturbing echoes' behind each day's attempt to greet the world. I return to that primitive and mysterious childhood realm each night. Jagged shards of time propel me downwards, out of control. I am repelled and shocked while glimpses of an exotic fairy beckon from the nearby shadows. Approaching, I find a desert stretched before me hiding in its vast expanse my earliest secrets. The realization that such dreams reflect primitive fears does not diminish my wonder. I still search for that eerie phantom of the

47

```
Adult life, childhood fears
(continued)
```

dark, the muse within who stirs my imagination. I suspect that the drama of this inner world can only be approached and never conquered.

I have learned to recognize the truth in my patient's eyes. Yes, I mirror his or her ideals and hopes, but in returning another's gaze, find reflections of myself. I take no consolation in finding still waters when looking for the God within. In such encounters, I feel driven to identify with the inner passion and hidden mystery of another. The power that I bring springs from my phantom muse, the hidden princess of the night. Even when afraid, I know that such vital memories must battle the emptiness of feeling that deadens another's vision. The possibility of the fire inside others draws me forward as a moth to a flame. My task as a therapist is to fan that flame into a passion for life. Anchored in the language of the present, I attempt to shape the experiences of their inner world to the concrete demands of therapy.

The great temptation is to ignore the reality of the other's experience. My own memories and inner journeys have left strong impressions and I react instinctively. After some years, I have learned to listen better, more quietly. What I hear most often is a tale of profound neglect during the most vulnerable time in life. It withers the soul and hardens the heart. This challenges my need to believe that life has an essential meaning founded on love. It takes me back to the nights of my own childhood when I would awaken with a fright, seeking comfort from my mothers. As I recall those moments now, feelings of sadness and isolation wash over me. I wanted both parents to be there, responding. Ever since, I have wanted to make things whole, to make it come out right. As a therapist, I seek to

engage the deepest layers of attachment. I find instead, that the embittered memory of another often blocks the way. It contradicts my purpose; it tears at my own memories and leaves me with no anchor, no starting point. Only then, when I am most confused and helpless, does my patient speak: "Now you know."

The mystery of our lives becomes heightened in the presence of another. I have looked up into the sky at airplanes passing by and wondered. I meet individuals and speak words that have little meaning. At times those closest to me seem like distant islands. What secrets dwell within giving direction to their lives? Does God exist or is life an illusion? Why must some impose their evil on others? The devil seems easier to define than a distant deity. It all comes full circle and meets in those experiences that so shape our perceptions of life, of others. I seek the truth hidden in the most sensitive desires of the soul, the whispered dreams of long ago. Then I become an intruder who rearranges the landscape and asks to be trusted. I justify the risks and the pain in the hope of a new life free of fear and dread. Perhaps it is also vindiction of that most precious time when I felt the anxious concern on my mother's face. At times I have lost touch with that feeling, but have sought to return to it in the lives of others. Like a voyeur, I peer forth from the inner worlds of those I have helped liberate. In listening and responding to their darkest moments, I have found myself returning to that small park on the border of my existence. This time, I run towards its shadows and embrace an unknown adventure.

William F. Kenny, a psychiatrist, is director of the psychiatric clinic at Greenwich Hospital.

Confused relationships reach down to raw nerves

By William F. Kenny

We were crowded into four small rooms. My mother and father, who did not get along, slept in different bedrooms, and the rest of us, like sailors on a ship, became their bunkmates.

When I left for college, I sensed that the world I would enter had little regard for the sound of such an intimate group. We fought and loved and cried within a few feet of each other. The words we used were visceral and direct. There was no ambiguity of feeling, and as a result, the atmosphere often screamed with intensity.

I have spent the intervening years wearing a more civilized mantle and yet carry within me the images and memories of that time. They form a backdrop to all that I do, and I find that I am constantly and instinctively seeking to touch the raw nerves of others.

Sometimes a couple will approach me with the problems they are encountering in a marriage. The initial descriptions are almost always the same, since each partner feels victimized and hopes for validation of his or her own views and behavior. I am asked to judge or to act as a referee and for the most part treated as a stranger who has just happened on a fight. I try to change the focus towards a more open-ended dialogue. There are raw nerves to be touched here, but not as long as the fighting continues.

I view all the quarrels and the hurting as halfway stations adopted as peculiar strategies to ward off any real danger. It is as if the two people, while seemingly different, had a secret world connecting them.

The surprising reality is in how few couples have been reared in an atmosphere of intimacy. There is a sense of bondage in each partner enslaving him or her in a ritual of disguised attempts to vindicate damaged self-esteem. At the heart of this dilemma lies a secret agenda on each side, unspoken and unthought. The driving forces of past attachments haunt each partner, raising the specter of fear and abandonment.

LOS ANGELES TIMES ILLUSTRATION BY RICHARD MILHOLLAND

As a result, acting becomes the dominant theme in a household emotionally flattened and geared to appearances. No wonder that after the early excitement of possession, the interpersonal space is quickly filled with noise and activity. The focus must inevitably shift outward, since the relationship cannot sustain the burdens discovered when time stands still. And our society, inamicable as it is to the sharing of self, arranges easy distractions. Career opportunities, peer group pressures and the lures of future accomplishments act like magnets attracting frustrated desires hidden in the imagination. As the partnership unravels, failed hopes stir embers of resentment and the only passion left resides in the agony of betrayal.

Listening to a couple in pain is like standing quietly in a hurricane. Everything is moving and there is no ground to shape individual identity. Accusations fly

49

in the wind, uprooting defenses and causing even greater wariness. My first task is to create a safe haven for the human voice. I do this by insisting that the couple accept me as a listener and not a judge, not an actor in their drama. I am curious not about how they hurt now but rather how they met and how each one's hopes were realized in the other.

In so doing, I encourage the memory of a time when coupling was a possibility. We then try to trace the obstacles to communication and the missed moments in time when even greater closeness might have arisen. I raise the possibility that there is something very valuable to be protected only by them. It is what they want to hear yet are afraid to risk and do not know how to achieve.

As a couple begins to look into the hidden nature of the expectations each has for the other, the focus shifts to the memories of child-parent relationships. It is almost as if the respective parents hover about and continue to exert powerful demands. Buried within these early memories there is often guilt associated with the failure to live up to parental hopes and desires. One's partner inherits the fallout from this experience and is expected to make up for this lingering fissure. Fantasies of love frequently contain elements of such a reparation and the hope that the other will make one feel whole and fulfilled.

When each partner brings to the union intensified needs for this kind of vindication, the burden becomes too great. The resulting feelings of failure dominate the couple, causing further alienation. As time passes, qualities once found attractive turn into irritations and frustrations. What was once seen as a complement to one's own limitations, now becomes an intrusion and threat. Compounding the situation is the feeling of being trapped in a relationship with someone who will never listen and never change. If only the other would become more open, less obstinate, things might change. Yet, the dilemma for each is that such hopes rest on unspoken fantasies constructed out of a need to repair wounds long forgotten. For as we delve into the memories and desires of each partner, it becomes clear that they are re-enacting a family drama embedded in their own character structures. The ensuing resentment merely serves to continue the bonds of hurt and deprivation developed in childhood. Moreover, as each participant strives to get such fulfillment through the other, he or she attempts to arrange things according to a

Confused relationships reach
down to raw nerves (continued)

pre-arranged script. This increases the sense of struggle and confuses the issues of just who is doing what to whom. Although each feels victimized, there seems to be significant areas of subtle collusion wherein both partners are busy arranging his or her own history.

I have learned through such experiences that one way of overcoming defensive behavior is to encourage each partner to share the past more fully with the other. In this way, lost dreams and past failures enlarge and deepen each individual's vision of the other.

Incompatible feelings succumb to the power of a common fantasy: the sense of being heard, of finally being understood. This looking into the other's soul has great fascination since it is so real, perhaps the only reality ever felt within. Somtimes the masks fall far enough to reveal ugly scars which can now heal in the light of a mutual embrace. Other times it is enough to discover that hateful passions do not kill. What each person is learning is how to use the silences amidst spoken words to grasp the situation of the other. As the other is felt in this way of listening, he or she is actually seen for the first time, without symbolic halos.

As we proceed from the establishment of a dialogue to the possibilities present in the moment, the outline of a clear identity separates each partner from the shadows. In the process, the need to please yesterday's commands dies slowly. Yet, the expansion of the ability to gaze into the eyes of another and behold an *I* and a *Thou* is a monumental discovery. It lifts each out of the failed search for love and provides a more certain account of meaning: to know that who I am matters to another and invites a mutual response.

This act of coupling is in turn an act of liberation from the bondage of the past. It needs to be learned in many cases because the environment in early family reltionships did not nurture the language of the soul. We live in a world that has almost obliterated the sound of intimate life. Its shallowness consumes individuality and leaves little room for any sense of significance. No wonder people hurt. No wonder the confusion.

We can, however, help individuals in pain by deepening their sense of themselves and enlarging the capacity to love. Ultimately, we cure ourselves when we reach for and touch our ideals.

William F. Kenny, a psychiatrist, is director of the psychiatric clinic at Greenwich Hospital.

● Greenwich Time, Wednesday, December 21, 1988 — **A15**

Moments of joy and pain at Christmas

By William F. Kenny

The Christmas season has always been filled with shadows for me. There was a time when I would look about and doubt my importance among friends. Sounds of laughter and expectations of a coming joy would only serve to heighten my sense of dislocation. Every year, I dreaded its coming and sought ways to distract myself.

Then, in a distant land, I found myself in the midst of an ugly war. For the first time in my life, death seemed a real possibility. The absurdity of such an ending brought home the realization that I must create my own destiny and separate from a past that offered no meaning.

In subsequent years I have anticipated each Christmas with measured caution. There have been moments of joy as well as pain, but always the sense that life is moving forward. I am surprised to find delight in the warmth of those who surround me with their love. It is a gift I sought but hardly imagined to be so broad and deep.

Greenwich Time

BOARD OF CONTRIBUTORS

My family life engages me deeply. Through the ebb and flow of our lives together, I have discovered strength in caring about others. This experience stretches back in time, erasing past sorrows. I wonder at the mystery and hold it close. I do not want to miss a moment of its richness.

I talk to individuals of their private despair. Curiously, they believe that the right words exchanged between us will explain away years of suffering. Like Merlin, I am expected to make pronouncements which carry magical implication. When I try to indicate that the business of listening stills any power to speak, there is often disbelief. I am doctor, I must know. Yes, the medicine man's garb casts its own shadows on the ground between us. Some patients use their symptoms to hide from themselves. They are afraid of human relationships and find it difficult to love. The tyranny of a heart frozen by fear is especially sad during a time of glad tidings. The sights and sounds of fellowship and good cheer seem like impossible achievements to the damaged ego. This can only serve to reinforce a sense of failure.

The images of Christmas unite birth and death in a unique tableau. We approach the Child in His crib with full knowledge of His death and allow the Agony to upstage this simple beginning. We are drawn towards the dramatic and away from the ordinary. Yet, His life lived in its full and glorious fidelity reflected a supreme confidence. Contrarily, the pain of isolation and depression expressed by many during this season often hides an anguished history. The frustration of the young child's yearning for love and attention creates a false perception of the world as cold and dangerous. Once blinded in this way, he or she begins to anticipate death each day. The growing alienation breeds envy of those who seem to enjoy life's moments of laughter. Finally, the anger becomes too much and the wish to exact revenge forces a withdrawal into guilt-ridden fantasy. The depression that follows often seems to be a distorted attempt to sacrifice the unwanted self in surrender to an angry God. In order to reach the child imprisoned within such visible agony, I find myself listening for soft whispers. Under the rubble of years of neglect lies a still beating heart which cries out, "Hold me, love me, I am afraid."

There is something quite beautiful in each human being which radiates under the gaze of another's concern. The self retreats before such care and hesitant expressions of feeling begin to find their way into the conversation. As these initial gestures find an appropriate response, the alienated self becomes a validated self. Along the way, outbursts of rage hang like familiar breezes in the air. Despite the pain, the attachment to a destructive past has a strong claim on the mind's eye. Yet, I believe that if I persist a while longer, the waves of fear will subside. Mostly, this is so. Sadly, sometimes I fail. In the process of encountering the hurt in another, I cannot always summon the will to engage my own hurting self. When this happens, I am lost at sea, unable to understand.

When I think of Christmas, I no longer feel the need to embrace the past. The present sounds of expectant joy reflect a triumph of love. I often discover such love only when resentment and anger have been acknowledged and rectified. However, this love speaks powerfully through the gestures of those in pain. I think of Christ born into an indifferent world. How hard He must have struggled to love the ones who rejected him. Somehow, He saw past the anger and derision and into the fear of twisted hearts. He embraced His own vulnerability and forgave them for being only human. As the carols ring forth with the Christmas spirit, the shadows recede and forgiveness reigns over the land. In the small corners where the light is weak, let us hope that the cries of the heart are heard.

William F. Kenny is a doctor at Greenwich Hospital.

52

Stir the imagination to deepen life's experience and texture

By William F. Kenney

The sidewalks of yesterday confronted me with hidden terrors. They stared up at me with gray impenetrable solidarity. In response, I would recite to myself stories I'd heard of the cracks which suddenly opened to trap the unwary. I took quite seriously the injunction never to step on them and thereby defined each day's adventure.

My brother, who was younger but more aggressive, added depth to my spectral imagination by chasing me among the shadows of a nearby graveyard. I would run through that grass and concrete checkerboard certain that he had changed into an apelike creature discharged from the bowels of the earth. Thank goodness it was a short distance to the street beyond, whose dangers were more under my control. Also, my mother and aunts would be near at hand, walking on their Sunday parade. It was very reassuring to find them amidst the strollers as if a statement by God Himself reclaimed the day. We always ended the afternoon at Schraft's ice cream parlor, another sign of the world's goodness. I knew then that security had its boundaries and that the horizon in my mind would always echo with childhood inventions.

One particular story that captured my spirit was "Jack and the Beanstalk." It was not so much his great prowess with the giant as the mystery of the beans that could transport Jack to another world high in the sky. I would look up at the clouds overhead and imagine roads and castles hidden in their midst. I would see myself walking towards an unknown ethereal land free from the constraints of a mundane world. Sometimes, even today, while riding in an airplane through thick clouds, I still wonder about life just beyond my awareness. For someone as hungry as I for enchantment, my religious instruction presented vivid detail.

I was taught by nuns who wore severe habits and seemed intent on frightening us into salvation. They told stories of death and damnation gleaned from seemingly intimate knowledge. Heaven, on the other hand, implied a life without end. In later years, school ushered in an all-too-demanding reality with its rules and consequences. I would rather have inhabited the playgrounds in the sky. The teachers I remember most were those who conveyed something of their own experiences of life

53

Stir the imagination to deepen
life's experience and texture
(continued)

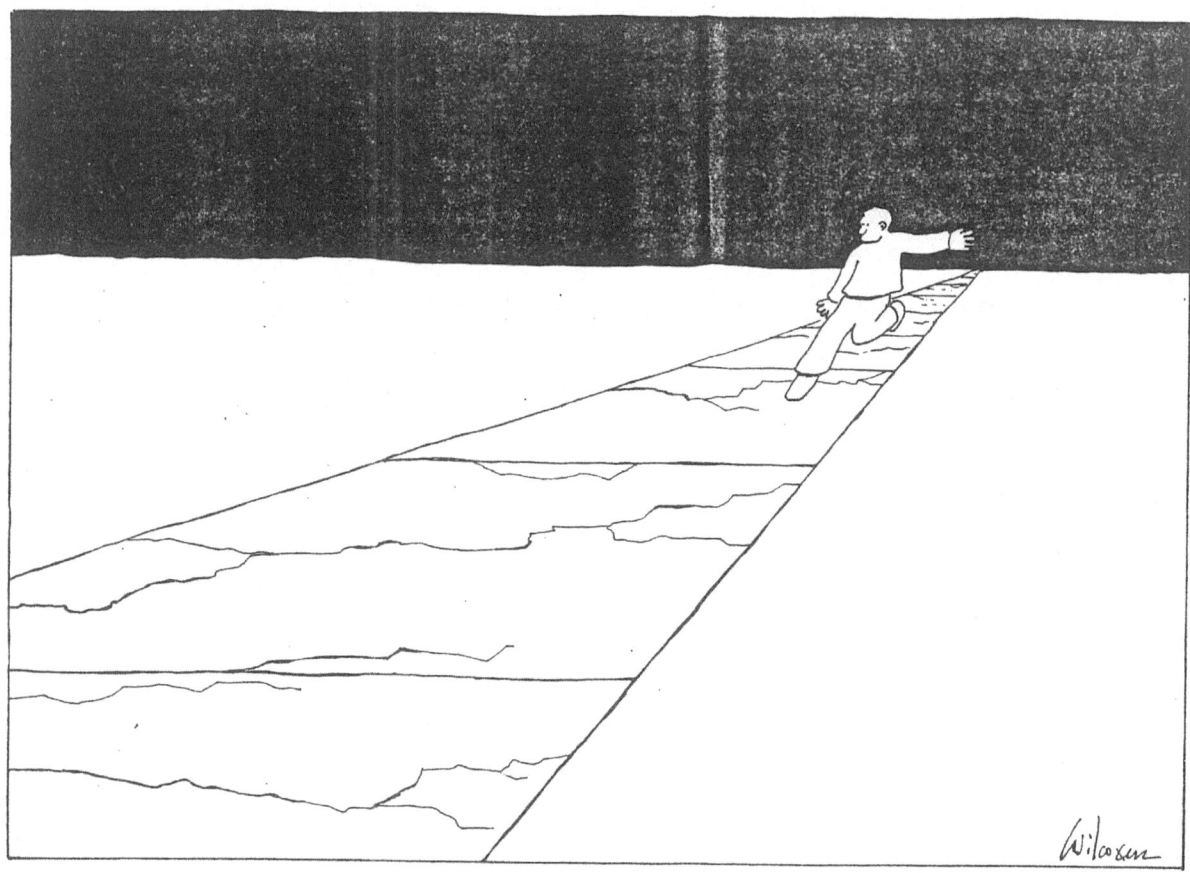

ILLUSTRATION BY CHUCK WILCOXEN

Greenwich Time

BOARD OF CONTRIBUTORS

which loomed just ahead, mysterious and forbidden. Every Saturday, I would go to the matinee movie and become enthralled with high adventure and evil villains. Monsters chased me in my sleep and I was defined more by the shadows than the sunlight.

Each summer, I would accompany my father to my grandmother's house at the seashore. It was always a time of great joy and freedom for me. I loved the smell of salt in the air and the sound of surf pounding the shore at night. Sandcrabs, boardwalk pavilions, ice cream cones and muscled lifeguards live continually in my mind. I remember the wonder of standing with my father at the railroad station. As the steam engine approached, its hoarse nasal whistle announcing its arrival, I would still myself with the power and the mystery. These were delicious moments full of the majesty of the world beyond and silent communion with my father. I grew up in an atmosphere of male innocence and fear. Women seemed more like creatures from another world than anyone I could identify. It was inevitable that my first love was more cerebral than passionate. We would sit for hours, lost in a crowd, discussing great ideas and only hinting at inner feelings. Then, one day, she was gone. For a long while, I looked for her face and a place to sit and talk again. The years have deepened my understanding and lessened the fears. I can look at a woman more directly and see the person there. Now, it seems that women have so much more to say than men. They have a greater feeling for pain and with that comes greater contact with the pulse of life.

It seems so long ago, this youth of mine. Yet, I cannot determine just when I left it

54

Stir the imagination to deepen life's experience and texture (continued)

behind. Was it my first love, so full of promise? I thought at the time that I could not survive the loss of someone who so filled the center in me. Yet I did struggle on without any clearer purpose than to survive. Leaving home became necessary when I realized that something inside me needed the taste of freedom. Each new school had its own battleground, and with success, I felt further removed from the neighborhoods of my past. I returned home less often and when I did, the sights and sounds hung in the air and did not dance. I had learned the ways of the world and buried the magical moments I had once cherished. I thought that I needed to overcome my fears and vanquish guilt. I gradually learned that these twins of the night harbored a rich lore of personal history. Only by plumbing their depths could I recapture the child in me and something of his world. This has opened my eyes to the hidden world in others. I look for signs of openness and vulnerability. This does not happen often in such a busy society. Ours is an ordered and rational world in which we hide our fears along with our imagination. We seek the protection of the group with its ritualized manners and narrow vision. We believe in the canons of dogma rather than memories of awe and uncertainty. We glorify sport while we sacrifice our young and deny our ignorance. Even our churches proclaim a God who comforts us with lazy platitudes.

I look about the landscape of a civilized people and see storms of protest. Drug wars and acts of senseless violence reflect a loss of joy and collective confusion. There is an increasing force to the discontent of the land. Yet, we continue to believe that our problems will disappear if we offer cosmetic answers. We substitute slogans for reality while our people are trivialized. When will our leaders learn that they must stir the imagination? There is a vast penumbra to our existence, filled with castles and magnificent creatures. When we pause to listen to each other's unique experience of this magical kingdom, our lives deepen and we touch one another. We come alive in the telling and rekindle the hope that someday our destiny will be as glorious as we had imagined.

William F. Kenny, a psychiatrist, is director of the psychiatric clinic at Greenwich Hospital.

• Greenwich Time, Sunday, May 6, 1990 — **A19**

On being a parent, and taking the risk to share the essential self

By William F. Kenny

My mother-in-law died on Jan. 17, 1990, in Montreal. When I last visited her, a few weeks before her death, she was a ghost of her former self. Her spirit, once bold beyond imagination, appeared only in the occasional moment.

I sensed her anguish even as she looked up and smiled at me. I tried but failed to utter words of comfort. She looked away. Even in the process of dying, she held back, giving little of her private self. She played her role to the very end and died as a lioness surrounded by her cubs.

In the days that followed, family and friends attempted to recall that special quality about her that immediately enlivened a room. Without her there to give shape to such memories, their efforts seemed feeble. As I moved from family members to friends during those baleful days, I thought to myself, "Who was she, really? What drove her? Why did she always hide her vulnerability? What kept her

Greenwich Time

BOARD OF CONTRIBUTORS

so young in life? Why did someone so hidden embrace others so warmly? Why did everyone love her so much?"

As a child, I thought of death often. I imagined what it would be like if my parents were to die. These were selfish thoughts since I was more concerned about myself than anything else. When my father died, I'd had years of separation to cushion the blow. In his later years, I found him full of resentment and unavailable. His character withered in stages until there was little left. His role in our family became more and more isolated. Yet his absence left a sharp void in my life. My earliest memories reflect the times that I felt closest to him. I

have always thought that I understood him. I still look for him whenever I return home. My mother, on the other hand, is all shadow. An only child, she lost her own mother when she was just 16. She does not speak of this time in her life very much. I do not ask. Her mind is much more worldly than mine, and yet she rarely leaves the security of her own environment. I think she believes that she has to be very careful in a dangerous world. Her life has been tragic and sad and yet powerful. Her influence on my life has been immense and to this day she remains a stranger.

I approach the middle years of my life with the gift of having known these two women. Their steadfastness in adversity provides an undertone, a spirit of perseverance. They are so different in their personalities and yet share an uncommon will that inhabits each moment and gives it purpose. Their children have been enlisted in this grand crusade, like it or not. This has produced mixed results and formed an uncertain emotional climate in each family.

Such powerful icons instill the drive to imitate rather than to individuate and reach out to the world beyond. Since the mystery of each woman has never been fully explored, we are left with the sense of something missing in our lives as well. As death has accepted one and whispers to the other, we, their children, yearn to touch them once more and conquer their pain and darkness.

We become parents before we are quite ready. I remember the birth of each of my own children as exciting yet anxious moments. I became in the process a public person, responsible for others. My private world seemed to visibly shrink. Through the years, I have struggled with the tensions inherent in the role of parent. I know that my children need all the strength and protection that I can give them. My instinct is to strive to fulfill my duties in every way possible. The image of two powerful women, faithful to their responsibilities and the roles assigned to them, haunts me. Yet, I do not want to die a stranger to my

children. My failings seem equally important if they are to understand me in any real way. Otherwise, all that I am doing is conveying a role that instills false ideals and promotes subsequent guilt. For these reasons, I think it important that they come to know that I can hate as well as love; that I have consistently fallen short of my ideals; that others have hurt me. This sharing of my vulnerability renews a bond with the first memories of my own father. His excesses seem to pale when I recall the warmth of his arms. My bitterness fades as I remember the lilt of his words. Most of all, I treasure the sheer joy of his imagination.

Being a parent is a difficult thing to be these days. We do our best to provide the right structure and to offer our love. However, if we take the risk along the way to share our souls with the ones we love, they will forever remember this as our most precious gift.

William F. Kenny, a psychiatrist, is director of the psychiatric clinic at Greenwich Hospital.

56

• Greenwich Time, Wednesday, June 19, 1991 — **A15**

Some men see 'Rabbit' in themselves

By William F. Kenney

A friend of mine died last year. Harry Angstrom, known as "Rabbit" to generations of John Updike's readers, appealed to me in powerful ways.

I first met Harry 31 years ago when I was a young man. I was in medical school and trying to decide who I was and what I was about. It was reassuring to discover someone like Harry. He too struggled to define himself. Now, at 55, I can still indentify with him and his flawed humanity.

In may ways "Rabbit" was not a very appealing figure. He was an unabashed womanizer and cheated on his wife. He failed as a father and indeed, never seemed to have matured. Yet, he took great pleasure in the little moments of life, whether it be the sun's dappled embrace of a flower or the invitation in a woman's eyes. His life did not have a grand design but was rather a series of moments in which his spirit soared. He spent most of his time in mudane efforts to get through the day.

Over the last three decades I have followed Harry Angstrom through good and bad times. His central failing was never to have explained himself to anyone. Those closest to him, his wife and family, remained as distant as friends and fellow workers. Perhaps he was afraid, as so many of us are, that no one would really accept him. Harry was often on the verge of expressing himself but would hold back our of fear of rejection or of hurting someone. He had good reason. Those around him were so concerned by appearances that all communication withered. They lived their lives along a flat plane, engaging each other as strangers. Harry was not strong enough to fight back and withdrew into himself. He tried to break our of his prison in affairs that only served to deepen his sadness. He died trying to recapture his success as an athlete on a basketball court. In one last physical act, he reached for the basket and fell to the ground.

I look at Harry's life and feel like a survivor. There is very little that separates us. I grew up in a family whose tensions flailed at us daily. I could do anything with a ball, whether to hit it, punch it or bang it. I inhaled sports as a quiet center of gravity amidst turmoil. It represented purity and completion, a kind of aesthetic comraderie beyond winning and losing.

For me, education would be the one great alternative to the limited horizons imposed by bright but wounded parents. As the world enlarged, so did I. Yet, a good part of me remained rigid and parochial. This was especially true of my experiences and views of women. They were objects of desire and unknowable. Then, one day, someone reached out and touched me. It was a beginning, an opening into the soft anf sensual side of myself. Since then, I have been able to risk much more. I feel fortunate to have had the experience denied my friend Harry.

I wonder how may men pursue their lives in isolation. They seek rewards that promise so much glory and then find themselves quietly forgotten. Much of this predicament comes from the ideas of masculinity developed early in life and continually reinforced by our society.

As male children we are prized for our toughness and athletic prowess. We do not cry after a certain age and are not applauded for being soft or sensitive. We are brought up to become warriors and workers. Simplicity and directness are considered distinctly male virtues while complexity and vulnerability are viewed suspiciously as feminine. The average man guards his private world tenaciously.

As the years accumulate, and the world no longer bestows its hurrahs, a man must reach much deeper into himself. This is what many men fail to do in their later years when work fades and career goals begin to pale. Frustration builds bitter monuments which often lead to despair. This is a trap "Rabbit" fell into that is so realistically detailed by John Updike. His life was a mirror of what can happen to a man when he is cheered only by admirers. He dies alone and misunderstood. Those lucky enough to have friends and family who insist on speaking to the boy within the man, grow and blossom.

I will mourn Harry Angtrom as a brother and remember his eye for beauty. What I love most about "Rabbit" it that he never gave up searching for the best part of himself. It is true that he remained an adolescent, but oh how human he was.

William F. Kenny, a psychiatrist, is director of the psychiatric clinic at Greenwich Hospital.

57

● Greenwich Time, Sunday, May 17, 1992 — **A17**

Building a bridge through therapy

GREENWICH TIME

Board of Contributors

By Dr. William F. Kenny

When I was a young boy, Saturday mornings seemed to last forever.

It was the time between the work of school and the morality of Sunday mass. Sometimes I would sleep quite late, as if to embrace an eternally warm space in which I could hibernate.

My mother would also relax her constant vigil over time and not bother to wake me. The only reason to get up early would be to meet on a ball field somewhere, an event I eagerly anticipated.

At first, my playgrounds were close to home, within shouting distance of my parents' apartment. Lunch and dinner were not at set times but rather whenever the other boys had to leave or when my mother would call. I was always too busy with the game at hand to notice anything else.

Looking back at those times, I remember the unlimited spirit of joy we all shared. Even after we moved on to more organized competition, the feeling that our lives were simple and harmonious persisted. As long as I could immerse myself in the boundaries of sport, with its clarity of meaning and promise of redemption through winning, life was eternal.

The afternoons were often spent at the local movie house. There I would sit in a magical black cloud lit up at one end by a glimmering fairyland of heroes and villains. I would go with my brother, but in those days almost the entire nighborhood would also be in the audience. We shared a common feeling of adventure and wonder at a world beyond our own experience. Each Saturday we would return to a new encounter whose risks were bravely faced and ultimately overcome. We grew up in a spirit of optimism, vaguely aware that someday we would move on to new playgrounds and leave behind the familiar faces of childhood.

Building a bridge
through therapy
(continued)

As I have grown over these many years and life has imposed its various choices, I have sought refuge in these memories. I love romance and am an inveterate movie goer. The real world often seems pale and much too limiting. The people I meet are intent on making sense of there lives and proving that they somehow count for something. Would they understand the need I have to immerse myself in frivolous fantasy? Do I really want to explain myself to anyone in particular? Would I not prefer the weird and wondrous images that cascade through my dreams? However, there is a certain hard edge to social encounters which does not allow for this kind of dialogue. The soft center of the human heart is well protected. There are occasional moments at a party, when I hear something more. It may be an inflection of the voice, a slight smile or a turn of the head. For me, this is the only moment of importance in a sea of noises. At these times I can risk bieng different and share something of myself. Such moments are few and this explains why psychotherapy holds such an appeal for me. It provides a healing space for the heart.

The business of therapy is very much a maternal act. Its drama focuses on the need to be understood and nurtured. However this understanding is not so easily accomplished. People have a way of disguising themselves and generally are unwilling to reveal their deepest

• Greenwich Time, Sunday, April 18, 1993 — **A15**

Building a bridge of commun[ity] for man, wo[man]

By William F. Kenny

Board of Contributors

I have always been haunted by the cracks in the sidewalk. I remember the stories in childhood that warned us they could open wide and become dark holes that would lead to the depths of the earth.

I secretly believed in these stories and studiously avoided stepping anywhere near them. Fear of the dark and the unknown seemed to be ever present and to inhibit each impulse. I looked for cracks where none existed. As a result, I anxiously embraced the ideas of sin and damnation that so permeated the atmosphere of an immigrant church.

The nuns taught us to regard desire as the enemy of the soul. Whenever I look at a childhood picture of myself, I wonder how I managed to conceal such struggles behind an innocent smile. Sex, of course, was the most feared aspect of reality, especially among the Irish.

Each Friday night the local youth organization would hold a dance for high school kids at the parish gymnasium. I would go there to meet my friends and hope to find the girl of my dreams. I was terribly shy and rarely talked to anyone.

It was especially difficult for me at the beginning of the evening when the crowd was sparse and there were a few girls present looking as lonely as I was. The idea of walking up to one of them and actually saying something seemed beyond me. I envied those who spoke easily and danced well. I found some relief in the adjoining ping-pong room, where I could dazzle other timorous boys with my skills.

Between games, I would go out to the dance floor and look for a face I might have seen earlier. Of course it was pretty crowded by then and my dream was always in the arms of another. At the end of the dance, I would walk home with the mystery and excitement of the night muted by my sense of failure.

During those early years, sex was the dark hole I desperately tried to avoid. I believed that I could rigidly control mind and body but never succeeded. This war with myself continued long into early adulthood and left its scars. I found it hard to form

As ur- till eir . I

longed to touch and feel a warmth that I knew existed.

Fear held me back and fear made a prison cell of my imagination. This was reinforced by a religion that

60

desires. This is especially true for those who have been hurt by individuals they have trusted in the past. For a long time, the issue of trust invades every word and each gesture of therapy. I often feel on trial, searching for some way to show that I intend no harm. In my early years as a therapist, I thought that this was enough. I felt that my desire to heal would be self evident and invite the trust that I was seeking. While this helped some, there were far too many who left my office feeling empty and not really understood. They demanded something more from me.

At first, I retreated behind the professional mask of neutrality until I realized that such a stance was cold and impersonal. It merely served to protect my own anxieties and reinforce feelings of deprivation. What I needed to do was to put something of myself into the response without losing focus on the unfolding needs of another. In a way this revived my own deeply buried longings to be held and reassured. I began to identify more with my patients' experiences and to share their pain. I found as well that when I could locate a common ground between us it would open up even greater depths. Invariably, these encounters served to validate that person's belief that he or she had a right to ask for something more out of life.

It takes a long time for scars to heal. It takes even longer for self confidence to take hold. I remember the arguments between my parents. They would suddenly escalate into anguished accusations of each other while I stilled myself with shame. Equally important was my anger at their indifference to my presence. I have been slow to give up these feelings. They have wrapped around my soul and stifled thought. Fortunately the love of others has given me the space and time to grow and feel secure enough to reclaim the magic of my childhood.

Building a bridge
through therapy
(continued)

Many people however, can not so easily escape. Their wounds are deeper, more searing. They repeat in their sessions with me the frightening effects of outright brutality. These early traumas have a very present reality and threaten to dominate the air between us. Yet, as the relationship flowers into one of understanding, I find myself encountering even deeper layers of my own memory. In these images I have cried out in the night and found the arms of my mother. She is alive and warm with a soothing embrace. Her words comfort me and the night seems less fearful.

Contrarily, the lack of such a reassuring maternal presence is often reflected in the stories of my patients. There is a deadening vacuum in the center of their existence. Sadly, they seem to have been raised by childish parents whose own needs diminished their capacity to nourish. Despite such deprivation, however, they remain mysteriously bonded to the past. I try to summon the strength to battle these ugly ghosts.

At times I question the whole process. If someone chooses death over life, should I not let him or her alone? I am too angry at my own past to allow such a defeat. It is my fight as well. Through this process of mutual identification, we begin to exorcise our shared demons. I in turn try to evolve a new and safer reality to replace this haunted dialogue. My task is no less than to fashion a new beginning, a life enriched with meaning.

Dr. William F. Kenny, a psychiatrist, is director of the psychiatric clinic at Greenwich Hospital.

Fear held me back and fear made a prison cell of my imagination. This was reinforced by a religion that viewed women with the mentality of the Dark Ages. It held that their proper place was to be either pregnant or behind cloister walls.

I still approach women hesitantly, but I have begun to see them more clearly. Now, when I meet a women, my first reaction is to notice her eyes.

There is a certain kind of look that invites directness and honesty. A smile on her lips heightens the occasion and promises an ability to laugh at herself. Quite often her first gesture establishes itself in my mind's eye and suggests gentle assurance.

I am invited by these impressions to communicate more of myself than I usually think possible. Yet, my vision remains a limited one, constantly needing help. A woman's sensitivity often bridges these embarassing moments with her understanding. When this occurs, a veil lifts and her face seizes me entirely. I am startled and retreat to a distance before I can appreciate the soft fullness of the woman before me. Again I search out her eyes. They dance and create a minuet of feeling between us.

I have remained an essentially private person sensitive to pauses in the rhythm of speech. In conversation, I scan the space between words and emotions looking for another's secret language. This is often revealed in unguarded moments when laughter and play fill the air.

I am always surprised to find how much alike we are when we tell our stories to each other. An abiding curiosity has led to a search for explanation behind the complaints that individuals present when they first enter therapy. As a therapist, I try to unlock the feelings trapped inside a person who seems tired and elusive. This involves a revealing of oneself through speech that often hides the burden of a wounded past.

During therapy, the words are difficult because they were born in a time of pain. I try to be reassuring and draw from my own history to reaffirm our common heritage. Small gestures will often signal unspoken communication. This silent language is elegantly reflected by a woman's hands. In the beginning, they are quiet, expressing her shyness with me. In time, they begin to speak and often prefigure the changes in her personality. Greater self-assurance is reflected in hands that become more feminine and sensual. They open toward me in ways that suggest acceptance. I find myself responding with greater authenticity.

We move from gesture to language in order to explore more precisely the unfolding of our shared perceptions of each other. I learn a history of the suppression of her spirit while she begins to trust me a little. We both learn that the land of our imagination touches at various and surprising points. As the relationship grows, our speech warms to friendship. When it comes time to say goodbye, I find myself drawn back to the eyes which now are alive with meaning. I find great comfort in having closed the space between us and for a brief time diminished our solitude.

William F. Kenny, a psychiatrist, is director of the psychiatric clinic at Greenwich Hospital.

Building a bridge
of communication
for man, woman
(continued)

Trying to fill a gap left by dad

By William F. Kenney
Board of Contributors

We gather together every other week in each other's homes. There are on average seven or eight on a given night as we meet to tell our stories. We bring to the evening our hurts, our sorrows, our anger and our joys.

More importantly, ours is a shared comraderie among a group of men intent on providing a place to soften life's burdens. This can be seen in the warmth of our greeting as we embrace each other's quiet smiles.

We are drawn to this arena by the desire to share our human dilemma and to go beyond the bullying corridors of achievement and competition that are normally our workplace. There is understanding and mutuality here as only a brotherhood of men can achieve. It reflects a common heritage and inspires easy laughter at our failings.

There is a sense among us that we have something to say that can only be heard and understood by men. This experience forges strong bonds that unite us in a very special way. It is a powerful journey. Along the way, I have felt each man's heart and become stronger.

As the evening begins, we take turns highlighting our concerns or the particular events that we wish to share. One or two issues will seem more pressing than others and will thus invite further discussion.

More often than not, our focus narrows to a personal conflict in a member's life. This usually stirs up in me considerable empathy since I have great difficulty in resolving such conflicts in my own life. There is an unresolved anger in all of us that escapes expression. We are in many ways too nice and reluctant to hurt others, especially our friends.

As children, we cherished our parents and were often disappointed in them. There is a void in our lives that marriage and family cannot entirely fill. We sift through the currents of our daily lives in search of an elusive meaning that will encourage us to become bolder. We listen to each other with great intensity, hoping to catch the missing piece from the puzzle of our lives. It is there deep down in the anguish of another that I begin to hear the echoes of my own past.

Images of my father beckon to me from across the years. He was a man gifted with superior intelligence and great charm. He could tell stories as only the Irish can, and my fondest memories are of lying in bed at night enthralled by his voice and magic. He seemed at the time to embody everything I desired.

As I grew older, my father did not grow with me. He remained firmly rooted in his own narrow world and distrusted the wider horizons that called out to me. He would invariably steer our conversations to himself and his own accomplishments and seemed little interested in what I was doing. Yet, I know that he often told others how proud he was of me.

It seemed that my father could not enter into any sort of mutual dialogue with me. As I look back, I realize that this would have made him feel vulnerable. He was a man who could not come to terms with his feelings and thus could never share his inner thoughts. He became bitter as the world and his friends left him behind.

By the time I came into possession of my own identity, the gap between us had grown too great to cross. He died a stranger to me, more of a memory than a friend. I have carried this relic of failed intimacy within my heart and always felt uncertain of my own value.

I look around the room filled with other men who like me, struggle to find their way. The stories I hear reflect each man's attempt to define himself more fully and to come to terms with the wealth of feeling inside him.

Their stories conjure up images of their own fathers and an equal sense of incompleteness. We have come together to grieve for the fathers we never knew. There is some sadness but much more longing to capture the strength hidden from us as children.

We now look to each other for the recognition so necessary in our lives and have learned to accept each other without pretense. We do not retreat from our neediness but rather celebrate our humanity. Perhaps we have come to love each other in a way that our fathers could not. And as we meet I imagine my father saying the things I have always strained to hear. It is a blessing, a benediction: "This is my beloved son."

William F. Kenny, a psychiatrist, is director of the psychiatric clinic at Greenwich Hospital.

Care and caring, then, now and tomorrow

By William F. Kenney
Board of Contributors

I remember when the family doctor would come to our house.

I had suffered for many years with bronchial asthma and from time to time would require an injection. As soon as the lungs cleared and my anxiety lessened, I would talk to him for a while about my hopes and fears.

He was a middle-aged man who seemed to have all the time in the world for me. I can still see in my mind's eye his warm and reassuring smile, which gave me the confidence that I so much needed. He served as a role model and inspired me to enter the field of medicine.

Recently, a colleague told me how important it was for him to elicit the cares and concerns of his patients. He was genuinely worried about the pressures that made it harder to listen in today's busy medical environment.

I think of this increasingly difficult dilemma as the debate about health reform reaches its critical stages in our society. The opportunity for human encounter, once so important, has been replaced by a modern medicine machine that raises the false hope of ultimate victory over pain and dying. Yet both physician and patient continue to find themselves feeling frustrated and powerless before the unyielding force of nature.

We can delay the end for a while and ease the suffering that our patients must endure. However, we can never completely conquer the dread march of disease as it claims its victims and finally catches up with each of us.

The physician's most important role is to share the burden of his patient's illness. This common identity enables the patient to truly reveal himself or herself.

It takes a while for both patient and doctor to get to know one another as fellow sufferers and to learn each other's true meaning. Paul Dudley White, President Eisenhower's cardiologist, said that the best medicine can only be practiced at one's leisure. I think he meant that the art of medicine must take time to evolve if we are truly to engage each other's spirit. And it is the spirit that heals.

The debate about health care reform has spread throughout our land and has in many ways polarized our society. The poor want to share in the benefits of the great society while the affluent wish to keep what they have worked hard to achieve.

The truth is that our country is not as wealthy as it once was, and we can not afford to pay for everything we want. Our leaders must make difficult choices and they are reluctant to put the real debate before the American people. Instead we have been offered various bureaucratic reforms that attempt to solve our problems through fiscal sleight of hand.

In the process, the individual patient is being removed from any personal relationship with his or her physician. Doctors and hospitals, on the other hand, have been seduced by the lure of big business and the promise of greater rewards resulting from the use of more and more technology. It is no accident that we are seeing the rise of mergers and acquisitions in the health care field. Medicine is a very big business these days. Somehow we have gone astray and lost the time to capture and hold in a healing embrace the human spirit.

I have worked for the past 16 years at Greenwich Hospital and found it to be a place where people still care very much about people. It has been a home for me and allowed me to spend time listening to my patients. Despite economic pressures, it has remained true to its mission to deliver quality care to all in the community.

I know doctors, who, like my colleague, take the time to listen and nurses and aides who go the extra mile for their patients. Greenwich Hospital has managed to remain a place where doctors, patients and staff have a personal space in which to conduct their business.

There has been a great deal of discussion lately about the hospital's future. Experts debate the merits of various plans. However, the hospital's infrastructure has been decaying for some time. The Benedict Building, which is to be replaced by the new hospital, is a failing monument of poor ventilation, inadequate plumbing and cramped space.

Logic dictates that we rebuild and create a modern structure that will help to continue a tradition of excellence. In this way we can preserve this home where there is the time and the opportunity for personal exchange and a healing spirit. My fear is that the Greenwich community will let slip away one of its greatest assets, and we will be left with the results of whatever our insurance technocracy decrees. At that point one's choice of doctor will matter little. All of us will be attached to machines that will determine our future.

William F. Kenney, a psychiatrist, is director of the psychiatric clinic at Greenwich Hospital.

64

Pieces for the Greenwich Time newsletter
by William F. Kenny

Part II Health Topics
1985 - 1987

Helping those who can't help themselves

Bill Kenny at work ca. 1985.

Greenwich Time, March 31, 1987

Facing cancer with dignity — and hope

By Dr. William F. Kenny

Once feared to the point that even its name was never mentioned, the diagnosis of cancer has changed in its implications during the past decade.

We now have open discussions with patients and the development of cancer-support groups. The cancer-treatment program at Greenwich Hospital has two oncologists as well as variety of supportive treatment personnel.

The cancer-support group itself is composed of patients in varying stages of the disease who meet on a regular basis to discuss common problems. A social worker from the hospital acts as a facilitator for the group and a source of information and moral support.

One of the obvious benefits from these meetings is the discovery that cancer is a multifaceted problem that takes different shapes and has a different and unique prognosis for every individual. It really does require a team effort to sustain the patient through the early stages of this illness and to offer a sense of hope and meaning in the struggle for survival.

One way of looking at the confrontation with cancer is to describe the reaction to such a discovery as a mourning or grief responses. There are five distinct

HEALTH VIEW

phases to this process, and the knowledge of each phase helps us to understand the cancer patient in a clearer light. While acknowledging a great deal of overlap from one phase to another, they can be fairly accurately depicted as the following: alarm, protest, search for meaning, despair and reconciliation.

The news that one has cancer initiates an intense alarm or fear reaction. This dread disease and its name directly attacks our sense of security and hope for survival. There is a numbing of one's entire being, and the instinct is at first to deny its reality.

At this time, some individuals characteristically engage in a flurry of activity in order to reinforce the idea that nothing has changed and that life goes on, as usual. For most, however, the reality is soon inescapable and deeper feelings of anger or protest follow. These feelings are sharper in those who are younger and whom this disease strikes in the prime of life. Such anger can be directed at God, faith, doctors and the world in general. This is a bitter pill and one that separates the cancer victim from the rest of his fellow human beings.

After the initial stages of alarm and protest, the patient with cancer must attempt to deal with the reality of his life as it is now threatened by grave illness. Very often such a threat stimulates an acute search for meaning and answers. This can take a variety of forms but generally this stimulates a search for new forms of treatment or radical cures.

There are a variety of cancer-treatment centers throughout the United States and the world that specialize in one form of cancer treatment or another. Some claim that patients will get better treatment at these centers because of their particular expertise. It must be kept in mind that the diagnosis of cancer is a generalized one and has to be looked at in a very specific manner in each individual. The outlook for surviv-

al and cure depends to a large extent on the specific kind of cancer, the time it is discovered and its location as well as the possibility that it might have spread to other areas.

Given these different factors, the outlook for any one individual cannot be compared to another, and each one's case must be individualized and evaluated by a knowledgeable physician.

As the search for answers and meaning reaches its culmination, there is a significant danger that despair and frustration set in. At this time, guilt about one's past and fears of bodily mutilation often dominate the individual's consciousness, threatening to paralyze all activity. It is at this time that the cancer patient is in most need of support from his or her family and can benefit from the kinds of groups that we have developed at Greenwich Hospital.

For most individuals who have endured the early stages of their illness, there comes a time when they must reconcile with its reality. At this time, the individual is quite open to the input of others. In effect, the patient has gone through his own individual panic and angry protest and has, by this time, obtained all he can from his own individu-

Facing cancer
with dignity
— and hope
(continued)

Cancer

■ Continued from Page B1

al search for answers. Depending on the prognosis and progress of the disease, that person will require more or less support.

As the patient comes to terms with the realities involved, there finally is a sense of freedom and the ability to accept what is inevitable. Through such acceptance the cancer victim learns to make realistic plans and to provide for the fullest life possible.

At this time the role of the physician — not just as a technical expert but more as a friend and guide — is extremely important because many cancer patients have become involved in a variety of medical treatments. It is important that there be one physician helping to organize the different aspects of the treatment process. It is essential to clarify and to make meaningful the events that are happening and the implications of different therapies. The cancer patient needs above all else a sense of continuity and meaning.

I remember clearly a time six years ago when we discovered that my mother-in-law had cancer. With the support of her family, she had radical surgery and follow-up chemotherapy. During this time there were all kinds of rumors as to what might or might not happen. However, my mother-in-law had the good fortune to have had an excellent physician who guided her through the maze of fact and fiction.

With strong family support she was able to take the courageous steps necessary to complete her course of treatment, and she now lives a full life. The past six years have been a very meaningful time for her, filled with many different individual and family events. If the initial stages of fear, protest and dismay had not been worked through, I do not think she would have faired as well.

She came to accept her illness and to accept the idea that she had to do what she had to do to survive. She did this magnificently, and we are all thankful that cancer is now a word that can be spoken and a disease that can be faced with dignity and hope.

————

William F. Kenny, M.D., is a member of the Department of Psychiatry at Greenwich Hospital and director of Greenwich Hospital's Psychiatric Treatment Center.

How to recognize, treat various forms of depression

By William F. Kenny, M.D.

Perhaps the single most frequent symptom that brings a patient to the psychiatrist is emotional depression. It can take may guises but most frequently appears as the feeling of hopelessness and dejection — usually accompanied by the tendency to feel guility about events from the past, and disturbances in both sleep and appetite.

The full picture of depression often takes several months to come about and by that time a patient usually has lost significant weight. Characteristic of the sleep disturbance is a tendency to awaken early in the morning and to feel most depressed during the beginning of the day. Sometimes this depressive mood improves towards the end of the day and is reflective of the

biologic or diurnal rhythm of depression. When a doctor sees the patient in his office there is often a telltale look which reflects what has been happening. The patient is slumped in a chair, speaks slowly and shows a retardation throughout all bodily movement.

This is a classic depressive syn-

drome. However, in many cases, it is not so apparent. Very often depression will affect the body in such a way as to produce disturbances in function. The patient might present himself to the doctor with vague abdominal complaints, headaches, difficulties in concentration and memory, constipation or generalized weakness and lack of energy. When a complete evaluation of the physical systems of the body reveals no specfic cause, the physician should be alert to an underlying depression manifesting itself.

Depression can take a variety of forms in terms of its course and outcome. The most common is that of a single or "major depression" which can appear at any age but most frequently occurs in the older age person. If left untreated, it can last from

six months to two years. It not only significantly incapacitates the person but also becomes a life threatening illness when it deepens and produces suicidal behavior.

This may be the only depression in the lifetime of the individual or it may signal the onset of a "recurrent depressive disorder" which can reappear several times during a person's life.

A third form of depression occurs as a prologue to a highly excited or a manic attack which causes an individual to engage in very bizarre behavior usually leading to hospitalization. The "manic depressive illness," now called Bipolar Disease, has a biological life of its own wth a tendency to recur every few years, causing untold

Please turn to **DEPRESSION**, Page B2

69

Depression

■ Continued from Page B1

havoc in the life of the individual and his family.

Once recognized, treatment of depression is relatively straight forward. Years ago, patients were subjected to dramatic procedures such as electroconvulsive therapy. While this method of treatment has gone out of fashion, in selected cases it remains an effective treatment with an almost 90% cure rate. Today, most depressions are treated with one of several antidepressant medications now on the market. The most common class of these are called Tricyclic Antidepressants. Their common names include Tofranil, Elavil, Norpramine, Sinequan, and Aventyl. Newer formulations of these drugs include Ludiomil and Asendin with a somewhat different chemical substance called Desyrel added to the list of currently prescribed medications. These drugs are quite effective, yet have significant adverse effects on various parts of the body. A physician will frequently try a patient on one of the antidepressants and switch to another if the patient cannot tolerate it. The most frequent side effects include dry mouth, some blurring of vision, as well as mild constipation. They are usually very transient and do not signify a need to stop

The use of medication to alleviate and cure the varieties of depressive illness has revolutionized its treatment. These drugs can often abort such an illness in several weeks.

the medication. However, individuals with high blood pressure and cardiac problems need careful monitoring by their physicians. Another important issue in the use of antidepressant medication is the interaction with the wide variety of other medications he or she is receiving.

A completely different class of medications used in the treatment of depression are the Monoamine Oxidase Inhibitors. Common names for these drugs include Pernate, Nardil and Marplan. They are as effective as the Tricyclic Antidepressants but need some special precautions. Several years ago, it was discovered that the Monoamine Oxidase Inhibitors interact with a substance called Tyramine to cause extremely high blood pressure. Since Tyramine is found in several foods, such as cheese, beer and wine, and in frequently prescribed medications it is important that the physician review with the patient the foods

to avoid and any other medications being taken in order to avoid this significant adverse effect.

In the last 20 years, the use of Lithium Carbonate has come to the forefront in the treatment of the manic depressive or bipolar illness. Lithium is not a drug in the usual sense of the term but rather, a salt. When Lithium is prescribed over several days and reaches a specific level in the blood it exerts a calming effect on the individual and tends to normalize extreme mood swings. This not only helps the acute attack or episode but has been instrumental in preventing recurrence of bipolar disorders. However Lithium must be monitored closely by a physician; its level should be drawn on a weekly basis for the first several weeks of treatment. Thereafter, monitoring can become less frequent. However the patient should notify his physician of any sudden changes in health status

or diet so that adjustments can be made.

The use of medication to alleviate and cure the varieties of depressive illness has revolutionized its treatment. These drugs can often abort such an illness in several weeks thereby eliminating months to years of turmoil and deterioration. It is important however that these different types of depression be accurately diagnosed since they require somewhat different approaches.

It is also true that many people suffer from milder versions brought on by disappointments of everyday life. In these instances where there is no significant change in the physical function of the body, and sleep and appetite is well preserved, it is most likely that the depression will either resolve itself or be significantly helped through supportive counseling and therapy. What must be remembered above all is that while the aura of hopelessness surrounds depression and its manifestation, the source of depression can be relieved and cured in the majority of cases with the resources now available.

•

William F. Kenny, M.D., is director of the Psychiatric Clinic at Greenwich Hospital.

Greenwich Time, April 16, 1985

Schizophrenia occurs in early adulthood, not childhood

By William F. Kenny, M.D.

A recent article by Dr. Leon Tec on the cause of schizophrenia in children raises some concern.

The term "schizophrenia" was originally coined to describe a group of serious illnesses arising in late adolescence and early adulthood. Tec extends this term to some type of psychotic reaction in and among children. This does not seem warranted nor is there any particular scientific evidence for diagnosing schizophrenia in childhood.

Tec points to a lower class family where the mother has been repeatedly hospitalized as possible causative factors. Again this is somewhat

confusing since most research on this matter does not list poverty, per se, as an etiological agent. It seems more likely that those individuals suffering from serious mental illness drift down the social ladder as a result of debilitating effects of chronic illness.

Likewise, the description of an overactive and sensitive child being vulnerable to the development of schizophrenia seems to raise more issues than are clearly resolved. Delicate and sensitive children are not necessarily vulnerable to the development of schizophrenia. The research that Tec cites indicating that 7 to 16 percent of children born to schizophrenics are likely to become schizophrenics themselves relates to the incidence of this illness at a much later age than childhood. Additionally, the strong genetic risks are manifest when both mother and father have the diagnoses of schizophrenia.

Finally, the diagnosis and label of schizophrenia in recent years have been questioned, and we are finding more evidence that individuals hospitalized for this illness, in fact, have suffered from profound disturbances in mood and have a much better prognosis.

In summary, while Tec quite rightly points to the interaction of constitutional and enviromental factors in mental illness, he has inaccurately attributed an illness that occurs in early adulthood to risk factors among young children. This would seem to me to raise unnecessary fears in the minds of the lay public.

William F. Kenny, M.D., is director of the psychiatric clinic at Greenwich Hospital.

71

Quality of life would suffer from tax panic

By William F. Kenny

We live in dire times. There is in this beautiful town a sense of panic. This has reached a crescendo as many have reacted to the prospect of an increase in property taxes.

The recent decisions of an RTM committee to recommend across-the-board cuts in the town budget reflect particularly thoughtless behavior. Inevitably, these reductions in money and personnel will affect services for the most vulnerable in our society: children, the poor, mentally ill, the elderly. Unfortunately, those whose lives need enrichment in order to participate fully in the American dream will be shunted aside to protect the interests of an uncaring and frightened affluent minority.

These reductions have been put forward without debate and dictated by individuals whose ideas of government seem limited at best. Their voices have been loud and shrill, claiming that the cost of the services is too much. They have not given us any standard of measurement. Instead of prudent deliberation, they have lashed out indiscriminately in all directions. They have decided for us, the citizens, without consultation. They have assumed that their narrow concerns have universal appeal. Yes, we are concerned about taxes. We are more concerned, however, about the quality of life in our town and that it continues to embrace all its citizens.

The proponents of this categorical budget slashing have been irresponsible in their actions as well as feckless in their thinking. They would decimate the structure and organization of the school system in the name of efficiency. They would do this without the slightest evidence of having understood the nature and function of the positions they would eliminate. They have targeted individuals whose careers reflect singular quality and effectiveness. They would eliminate services for the needy under the pre-

text that we can not afford to increase the tax burden. They have lost the sense of a social contract that each of us must accept if we are to remain a great nation. All this has been done in haste and dominated by the views of a few strident individuals whose interests are simply to stand still.

It is particularly distressing that such voices of discontent have gone unchallenged by the town leadership. While there have been thoughtful comments by various department heads and interested parties, our selectmen have been conspicuously silent. This is a time for moral leadership, not political complacency. Our leaders should not be cowed by the simplistic solutions of those who would economize at the expense of quality.

The future of Greenwich is too important to leave it in the hands of the merely pecuniary guardians of the ledger. We need our leadership to encourage a responsible debate on the issues and to create a climate in which our vision is not clouded by fear.

Greenwich has been a shining citadel, a marvel of diversity, a truly civilized arena. We trivialize its meaning when we are silent while others in their panic cry: "Enough, enough." Let us rather choose a more eloquent discourse where reason and common sense prevail. Let us as a body politic choose to preserve and build for a future in which we are proud of our accomplishments. Let us keep Greenwich a great place to live rather than a sad monument of frozen aspirations. We must allow hope to overcome fear.

William F. Kenny, a psychiatrist, is director of the psychiatric clinic at Greenwich Hospital.

Memories

Childhood

My earliest memories of childhood reflect persistent confusion. I was exquisitely sensitive to my surroundings and keenly aware of my parents' limitations. In many ways they seemed childlike and self-centered. They had frequent verbal as well as physical arguments, and it made little difference whether I was present. Although both were bright and sensitive they were totally unaware of each other's world. One time, after reading a book on sex and biology I confidently went to my parents with questions; their response was to look at each other and giggle. After a few such encounters I began to look else-where. Nevertheless, those were years of love and contentment. Just before World War II when I was two, we moved into an apartment building. It was a new complex designed by architect Ernest Flagg to accommodate a burgeoning middle class. In many ways this was a fairyland for families with children. Nestled among the buildings were a swimming pool, tennis courts, an auditorium, a bowling alley and a restaurant. We had a two-bedroom apartment which seemed very special. My mother sent me to the nursery school located on the ground floor of our building. Music was a daily part of the two-hour program. I especially remember our teacher, Miss 'Accordion'. She was warm and attractive and I loved her so. At night, I would dream of an Indian princess riding bareback on a mighty white stallion. The children I played with were white, Catholic, Protestant and Jewish; there were no black children. These were carefree days of strong friendship. We looked up to the older boys, three to five years our senior -- our teachers in many ways.

Shielded from the ravages of war, we romped in this magical playground. My parents as well seemed to prosper as they enlarged their family to include five boys and a girl, my siblings. My mother was a bright, warm woman with jet-black hair, sparkling blue eyes and an easy laugh. She graduated from a prestigious girls' high school and became a fine pianist as well as a good portrait artist. Yet she carried inside her the loss of her mother who died suddenly from Diphtheria while they were visiting family in England. Upon her return, motherless and needy, her father's unexpected marriage to a younger woman was badly timed. An only child, the experience of living with a new stepmother and her son, an unanticipated stepbrother, fed her insecurity.

At some point as things unraveled between my parents, my mother began to drink heavily and put on weight. Yet she was a social being who made strong friendships. She would regularly meet with the other mothers as they pushed their baby carriages around the tennis court or as they fed the communal washing machines. She loved babies and young children, often protecting us from the nuns who taught at the local parochial school. This was especially important for me when the nun in grade one told me that I would surely go to hell because I was left-handed. My fearless, non-Catholic mother marched up to the school and challenged that nun; she never dared bother me again. My father was smart, athletic and attractive with curly blond hair. Being the youngest child of a prominent Irish-Catholic family, he was very spoiled. He never finished high school and spent most of the time driving fast cars and playing golf.

My father read stories to me from the Arabian nights and other fairy tales, telling these stories with great fanfare and imagination. My favorite story was the Brave Little Tailor. The story is about a humble tailor who one day swats seven flies at once and who put a sign in his shop window proclaiming that he had killed seven with one blow. Now the wary townsmen took this to mean he had killed seven angry giants who lurked outside the village. They pleaded with the tailor to protect their town. The tailor accepted the challenge and set out to outwit the monsters. I would plead with him to tell this story over and over again. He would play catch with me and throw hard pitches; it was thrilling. He also taught me to play handball at the outdoor courts adjacent to the auditorium. I wanted nothing more than to please him. Yet, as I approached adolescence my father drifted towards my older cousin and his friends. He would fix their baseball gloves and hit balls to the outfield with his bat. I felt rejected and abandoned but kept it to myself. I did not understand why he needed their adulation. I also wondered why my father never joined a team or related to anyone in his peer group.

Around this time my parents fought more frequently. Their arguments would erupt suddenly for no apparent reason while I had a friend over. I was embarrassed and angry with them for their immaturity and lack of sensitivity. Their fights became more frequent and more physical. My father often invited the older boys to dinner for drinks and cards at our apartment. I could hear them all laughing as I climbed into my bed at night. My mother Dorothy, whom they called 'Dot', was the only woman present. I could hear her laughter as well. As World War II advanced, many of these boys were drafted. My mother sent care packages and letters to them. My father did not go to war because he was head of a family with young children. I remember feeling somewhat guilty about this and our apparent safety at home. We had a victory garden, which he cared for. When these young men returned from the war, they thanked my mother profusely for her letters and kindness. A few years later my mother, who had been in much pain and discomfort for some time, went into hospital to have her veins stripped. My father promptly took to his bed clamoring for attention. Years later my father became seriously ill and was hospitalized. I tried to comfort him as best I could. I also encouraged him to transfer the money in his bank account to my mother. To my surprise he did.

I was an anxious and obsessive child; I counted the captions in my comic books to ensure that I had read everything correctly. I developed asthma and frequently wakened in the night gasping for breath. My mother was always there to comfort me, holding me on her lap and stroking my back to help control my breathing. It strikes me that she was always there for me, fighting teachers, attending plays and travelling to my high school to meet the principal. I can feel her warmth to this very day. When I was in Vietnam, she sent me care packages and letters of support. In later years she travelled to California and Switzerland to keep contact with her children. I recently unearthed a picture of my mother sitting with my father, leaning back as her arms surrounded him. She is beaming in triumph.

Education

In high school, I began to distance myself from my family and neighborhood. Having passed a rigorous entry exam, I won entrance to Regis, a prestigious boys' Catholic high school on Park Avenue in Manhattan. Every student, rich or poor, attended on scholarship, which made for a very competitive environment. There were two tracts: classical, with Latin and Greek, and Science. I chose the classics, which steered me towards the arts and literature. The students came from various parts New York City with their equally different backgrounds. The school was very strict about punctuality, which was stressful for me as I had an hour's trip on the subway from my home in Brooklyn.

I worked hard and excelled in this environment. While there, I met a man who profoundly liberated me. He was the Jesuit chaplain at our school and a father confessor. He understood my sexual anxieties. He encouraged me to trust more in my own goodness. After completing high school, I was one of five from Regis who managed to win a competitive scholarship to St Peter's College, another Jesuit school. We all did well academically and became leaders in drama, the college newspaper and debate. There I found intellectual freedom in the study of philosophy. I began to see that there were other ways of understanding the world. I was particularly moved by the existential philosophers who emphasized the strength to be free of despair and to shape the future. In my last year, I became interested in the peculiar illness of schizophrenia. My supervisor, a professor of psychology and an Italian immigrant, referred me to the work of Silvano Arieti, who clearly described the peculiar thought patterns of schizophrenic patients. As a result, I wrote my senior thesis on their profound confusion. This was my first introduction to the world of psychiatry.

Upon graduation, I moved to Montreal to study medicine at McGill University. At the airport leaving for Montreal, my mother, ever caring and suspicious of air travel, managed to board and inspect the plane to make sure it was safe! I felt totally alone as a newcomer to Montreal with its large French-speaking population and overwhelmed by McGill University, a huge complex with several thousand students. On my first day I walked for hours looking for lodging. I finally found a French family with a room for rent. I stayed with these lovely people for the next four years, but sadly never learned their language. My first year was a challenge but I did well. My teenage sister took her first plane ride when she visited me in my second year. It seemed at that time a courageous thing for her to do and I was thrilled to see her. I showed her Montreal, took her to my favorite restaurant and to the theatre. I felt lonesome after she left. In my third year, several of us took a retreat at a monastery outside the city. While there, the retreat master, a Jesuit priest, confronted us with our faith. He suggested that if we had serious doubts about Catholicism, we should try other avenues of thought and religion. Needless to say, I held onto my faith, but the door had opened. It was the beginning of the voyage that sent me down the road that I am still travelling. *It is one of exploration of who I am, where I came from and where I shall go.*

During medical school, I spent summers at my parents' beach house. They seemed to be more relaxed and less angry there. My father took to fishing at the shoreline each night. He seemed lonely but often engaged in conversation with other fishermen scattered along the beach. My mother blossomed socially and made new friends. I was a good swimmer and became a lifeguard. After three years, I was named captain of the guards. This involved roaming the beach, making sure each guard was alert and focused on the water. I felt responsible for the safety of all the bathers who came to this beachfront. When not roaming the beach I sat on an eight-foot guard chair scanning the water and feeling important, keenly aware of the groups of young girls who usually came to the beach. They were friendly and would often come up to my chair to ask for directions. Painfully shy, my response was always businesslike and short in comparison to the other guards who relished this interaction and saw it as an opportunity to meet someone. I was particularly jealous of one of the guards, Pete. He was tall, dark and handsome -- a Greek God, who would carry a yellow rubber ball, pass by a group of girls sitting on a blanket and throw the ball which would just happen to land in their midst. He would then approach the group to ask if anyone had seen the ball. This always resulted in amiable chatter. I was always jealous of Pete, wishing that I had the nerve to interact in some way with these young women. At night, I would go down to the pier behind the local luncheonette with my friend Gene. It was a dark spot and there usually was music and the opportunity to dance to Peggy Lee, singing "Lover". I would often walk home filled with desire and longing for someone.

Those summer days flew by while my shyness imprisoned me. I watched others embrace freedom while I merely fantasized. By chance, I met Joan while attending a conference on modern philosophers. She was pretty and very bright. Most importantly, she seemed interested in what I had to say and how I thought. We exchanged ideas, sometimes argued. Still, we saw the world from a similar vantage point. Her face, her smile, her very existence enveloped me with hope. When suddenly Joan disappeared, I phoned her, wrote letters and even contacted her parents. They were evasive and offered no help. I was crushed and lost. Then, a few months later, Joan wrote me a letter apologizing. She had kept secret from me the extent of her intense desires and had entered a religious order of nuns. I was devastated and alone. It took some time but I finally moved on. I turned back to philosophy and penned the following:

Time is but the whimpering protest
Beneath a solitary stone
the lion in the field the sun
Melancholy brown gay blue
attest the presence but do not speak
I faced with emptiness surround
confuse my all too self with it
but death encircles
a lost love retreats from shadows
too soon and I become

In my last year in Montreal, I met Susan, a nursing student who had emigrated from Belgium. I was at a dance at her school when Susan came up to me and asked me to dance with her. There followed an intense courtship as she both frustrated and fascinated me. Her views were different and challenging. She pushed me to open up and share more of myself. At the same time however, she was heavily involved with an older married man. We met for the last time at a favorite restaurant. During dinner, her eyes were intently focused on me and I felt her love. However, with tears in her eyes, she said she could not leave her paramour. Out on the street, Susan turned around, still crying, and quickly walked away. I felt numb and in pain for a long time. I would imagine her on the street or catch a passing shadow only to see that there was no one there.

Residency

I graduated from McGill Medical School in 1961 and obtained my training at St Vincent's Hospital in New York City. I had thought of pursuing a psychiatric residency for some time. The Irish Catholicism of my childhood remained with me long into early adulthood. Sexual pleasure of any kind stirred the fires of hell. Medical school and more importantly my time at the hospital, enlarged my perspective and softened my fears. Yet, even the young nursing students who followed me on rounds seemed more mature than me. I dreamt often and slept poorly. At the time, I had a heavy schedule of severely-challenged patients and was especially interested in schizophrenia. I brought my early studies to bear on this strange illness and tried to understand their struggles. We did not know how much was biological or psychological. What I could understand and feel was the confusion, pain and utmost honesty in these patients. We had new medications such as Thorazine, which did reduce hallucinations and agitation, but flattened affect. The best and most humanizing treatment however, was the ability to keep a patient in hospital for several months. My unit housed around twenty-five individuals with varying complaints and forms of illness. However, we were able to develop a social structure with community meetings and frequent support from nursing staff, art therapists and clinical psychologists. We learned about the power of the group and the social forces so dominant in their lives. It was a humanizing experience for the patients as well as myself.

One of my assignments was to spend some time at a dementia unit in upstate New York. When I walked onto the floor for the first time, I was confronted by a group of women sitting separately, each staring blankly ahead. I did not know how to engage with them in their isolation. I decided to gather them in a circle and bounced a volley ball off their heads. There was not much response. However, one patient was quite verbal and I managed to converse with her. I would ask why she was in the hospital and she responded saying she was sick. I would then confront her and say she was not so ill and could return home. Occasionally, I would again throw the ball at her and she would swat it away. After several weeks it was time for me to leave. As I walked off the unit this angry, determined woman sat down at the piano and played "I Love You Truly".

In my first year of psychiatric residency I met Bob. He was unusual and funny and in him I found a comrade-in-arms. We laughed and grappled together, forming a friendship that literally changed my life. He was the gateway to a social group that still endures. We shared an apartment with three other men on the upper east side of New York. Bob's great gift was his relish for adventure. Many summer forays were spent at his family's beach compound on the North Shore of Long Island that had a tennis court where we often played. We were part of an Irish Catholic community that interacted socially with women of similar backgrounds. It was a safe environment for me while I tried to navigate the world. In our third year of residency, Bob and I travelled to Washington to discuss our military deferrals with the commander of the US Army Medical Corp. On the way there, Bob regaled me with his expectation of being sent to Hawaii and great adventure. I worried. There was dead silence in the room when the General announced that I was going to Vietnam and Bob to Korea. Bob adapted well as a psychiatrist in a foreign land, making friends and winning various tennis titles. When I was six months into my stay in Vietnam, Bob wrote me a letter offering to parachute behind enemy lines. Such was his fantasy and exuberance. We managed to team up again on our return to America and found a duplex apartment on the west side of New York. We enjoyed this magnificent abode with two friends and joined a circle of young males searching for the good life. In many ways we grew older together. Our birthdays came a few months apart and we celebrated our 70th with approximately 60 friends and relatives on the deck of a McAllister tugboat that cruised New York City harbor. It was a glorious, sunny afternoon as we circled the Statue of Liberty while a guest sang in her beautiful soprano voice "The Star Spangled Banner". We danced and we dined as Bob embraced his role as an impromptu Master of Ceremonies and sang "happy birthday Bill", and I also made a few remarks to the guests. My fondest memory of Bob however, is of the time we gathered with good friends at his summer home as he led all of our children to the beach, merrily singing like a veritable pied piper. They called him Bob Daly while they addressed all the other adults as "Mr." or "Mrs." Sadly Bob died a few years later from lung cancer.

Whenever we gather with our friends Bob's name inevitably comes up and we reminisce. In his memory I wrote this epitaph:

Gone, gone, gone. The pied piper of our dreams
Ripped from us by a god indifferent to our dreams
We had hoped for a miracle that never came
While he knew instinctively the end was near
In the hospital, he spoke of doctors, tests and drugs
Yet always came back to the reality we avoided
But we left and the nights were long and alone
This man, this brother, our constant comrade
Strode through our lives with the force of a lion
While we struggled, he roared. The future beckoned
With images he created and we laughed along
Willing to believe that life could be enchanting
In his presence we forgot ourselves and were less alone
This was his great gift to us, his love for us, his friends
He was never happier than to be among us confronting
Our concerns, regaling our fears half smiling to himself
With him the future always seemed possible, within our grasp
He is gone now and there is an aching in our soul
For the man who so enriched our lives
His stories, his laughter, his merriment are gone now
And emptiness invades our memories
How can this be? where is the meaning, the future?
We search for him in our dreams in hopes of peace
And hear again his roar: life is for the living not the dead
To love despite fear, to enjoy despite pain, to sing again
This is his final gift to us his forever friends.

Army Service

I entered the US Army but was deferred from service until I finished my residency. I was determined to fulfill my obligation to country, in some sense recompense for my father's escape from service. I spent 13 months in a war zone as a captain in the U. S. Army Medical Corps. I came to Vietnam after a long plane ride with a stop in the Philippines. As we approached Saigon, now called Ho Chi Minh City, the pilot told us that we had to land swiftly to avoid enemy fire. When we arrived, an army colonel told me that I would initially go to a MASH hospital, just outside the city. It was a tented complex in the midst of a jungle and served as the evacuation center for the wounded. I slept in one large tent holding some 20 soldiers with a mosquito net above my bed to prevent catching Malaria.

I did not come down with Malaria but did contract amoebic dysentery. I woke up each morning to busy helicopters landing one after another to unload their human cargo. I was a watcher more than a participant. Everyone involved walked with a purpose, a casual competence. I did not know just how I might fit in. At night, I looked up to a black and velvet sky sprinkled with a million stars that I could almost touch. There was an eerie silence to it all and I wondered what the mornings would bring. While there, I became friendly with another captain, a psychologist attached to the hospital. He told me that each night he left the camp to be with his wife, who had rented a house in a nearby city. I thought this was strange as it was supposedly forbidden. I found out much later that our Ambassador to Vietnam had done the same thing. After two weeks I was dispatched to Saigon, the capital of South Vietnam. It was a beautiful city that still retained many aspects of the culture imprinted by its French colonials. I occasionally found the time to play tennis at the Cercle Sportif. I played on the hot red clay with another army captain who was much better than I. The Vietnamese people were, and are, handsome, intelligent and proud of their long heritage and history. In the center of Saigon there was a large, sprawling market dominated by a fantastic array of flowers. It was adjacent to the Catholic cathedral and a shrine where Buddhist monks were occasionally spotted nearby, walking with their heads bowed intent on their meditation.

I made friends with two other physicians and we rented a small Villa from a Vietnamese army Major. He and his wife lived in an apartment above their garage. We would occasionally see them walking, always with his wife a few steps behind. We managed to hire a friendly young Chinese girl to cook and clean our house. She was amused by our easy-to-prepare western breakfasts of cold, packaged cereal. She was more comfortable with our evening meal when she could cook a fresh chicken, according to her culture, that she had just killed by wringing its neck. While there I spent a good deal of my free time going to the Army PX where I bought many discounted items. At night we went to Chinatown. The Vietnamese were afraid of the Chinese and resented them. They were the merchants and the bankers of the Orient. We often visited a well-known Chinese restaurant. The owner was an elderly Chinese woman who engaged our attention with stories about her son who was attending MIT in Boston. She was saving all her money to support him.

One of the many troubling circumstances in this war was that while we safely viewed the war from the rooftop of the REX -- the most popular hotel in Saigon, we were provided an extra cost-of-living allowance for living in town. It had a large restaurant that catered to American soldiers. After dark we would walk out onto the balcony to watch the war, the fireworks from the guns some twenty miles away. Despite a veneer of civility and camaraderie, the prospect of death surrounded us. There were soldiers with machine guns standing guard at every hotel and important building. Soldiers would often enter a bus to scan riders for Vietcong sympathizers. I slept with a loaded 45-caliber pistol under my pillow. One of my most somber memories was the sight of Vietnamese women carrying buckets of sewer water to be boiled at home for food. Amidst the turmoil I turned to the existential philosophers I had read in college, especially Karl Jaspers. He pointed out that we could only find ourselves through adversity.

I was attached to the 17th Field Hospital as its only psychiatrist. My daily routine was to drive on my motorbike to the hospital some 15 minutes away. I divided my time tending to a four-bed inpatient unit and my air-conditioned outpatient office across the street. Most of the soldiers suffered from anxiety, depression and the lonely separation from family. Alcohol abuse became an avenue of escape from the drums of war. The scourge of drugs had not yet become visible. I remember one patient in particular who had suffered from shock after his quarters were blown apart by mortar. He was suffering from acute agitation, his behavior almost delusional and was requesting that he be evacuated to the United Nations in order to appear before that body. He wished to lead a battalion and return to Vietnam to kill everyone in sight. I sedated him heavily for one week before he returned to his unit. When I was leaving Vietnam months later, I met him at the airport. He told me to my surprise that he had been put in charge of scheduling for the departing planes.

Halfway through my tour, I left for Bangkok, Thailand for "rest and relaxation". It was a very large city, similar to New York with large buildings and teeming with people. The Thai people are exceedingly beautiful and gracious. I wandered through the jewelry and garment centers and arranged to be fitted for a new suit. However, I was alone and unsettled with the prospect of returning to war. One night, I went to a nightclub, which featured Gladys Knight and the Pips. While eating dinner, I heard a soft voice say: "Hello, may I sit?" I looked up to see a gorgeous, smiling woman who spoke perfect English. I invited her to join me at dinner and we had a terrific conversation. She knew the city well and offered to guide me. It was a glorious five days full of sunshine and laughter. On my last day, she took me to the Asian Games full of splendor and excitement. I left Bangkok with a lighter heart and renewed spirit.

Despite the somber atmosphere, morale was high and cemented by the bonds of brotherhood. I remember a soldier who was severely wounded and evacuated from the front lines. Although married with several children, he pleaded to be returned to his comrades. At times the absurdity of the war became apparent. In one instance, a friend, an army captain assigned to shepherd a Vietnamese company in search of the enemy, determined, while on patrol in the middle of the jungle to have everyone stop, sit and listen to a World Series game. I was especially envious of the doctors who managed to get assigned to the planes carrying wounded soldiers home. The upsurge of drug abuse and corruption was not yet apparent. Home seemed far away.

Back to Civilian Life

My experience in a combat zone and the specter of death inspired a decision. I felt that I had to understand my struggles and move on. When I returned to America, I entered therapy and was referred to an eminent analyst who had written several books. I respected this man very much, especially his intellect. He was a strict Freudian who sat behind me as I lay on the couch for my tri-weekly visits. I was nervous at first but quickly felt a new sense of freedom. I reported vivid dreams and expressed the fears that kept me prisoner. He said little and at times I imagined him asleep. I respected him yet felt anxious in his presence. I wondered about his sexual orientation and whether he was married. I resented it when he answered brief phone calls during our sessions but I never protested. I knew that he was involved in arranging tennis tournaments but I never shared my own passion for the sport. At one point, I accused him of not understanding my Irish Catholic background. He reacted and challenged me to explore my roots and Irish history. This led me to Yeats, Shaw and Brendan Behan. Throughout the analysis, I reported my dreams. As we progressed, I experienced a bizarre array of images and emotions. I was especially frightened of a fantasy in which he was sitting behind me and smiling. I never shared that with him. I talked a lot and dreamt a lot and in many ways felt freer than ever. In my third year of analysis, I was bedridden with severe infectious mononucleosis and missed several weeks of therapy. I was surprised when he charged me for the appointments. I paid him but felt disappointed and angry. I realized then, that though very learned, he did not have a heart. It was time for me to end therapy and move on.

I met the love of my life Lynne through friends I knew in New York. Although dating other people at the time, we had long conversations about life and books. She too knew the works of Hugh MacLennan. She was Catholic, Canadian and very beautiful. She also was thoughtful and determined. Lynne conveyed a depth and intimacy that reached into my soul. I finally got the courage to ask her for a date. Together we found ourselves creating our own little bubble of joy. Lynne was an avid student of art, eventually getting her MA in art history. We often visited the many art museums and treasures available in the city. When I encountered the paintings of Picasso, Matisse and especially Pollock or Monet, it was for me an explosion of visual emotion. I remember especially walking down a street in New York's Little Italy one sunny fall afternoon, early in our courtship, nonchalantly feasting on the most delicious Italian pastry I had ever tasted. The night before, we had dined at a special restaurant in Greenwich Village. We arrived around 7 PM and talked through the evening over Canard à La Montmorency and a bottle of Châteauneuf du Pape. When I finally looked up it was 11 PM and we were the only ones left in the restaurant. We knew then that we would have a life together. We met in September and were married three months later on December 29, 1969. My parents did not come to our wedding for reasons unknown. I knew that initially my mother resented Lynne but this changed when our first child, William, was born. It was love at first sight as she took her day-old grandson in her arms and said: "I have been waiting for you all my life". Our marriage of 50 years has been the result of mutual trust and admiration. Lynne's love and steadfast faith in me has been a beacon ever present in my life. She followed me in my travels adapting along the way and never complaining. She has been a gift that I never envisioned. Years later, I wrote this homage:

I see your face in a picture smiling with all
hope captured in your eyes so joyous
and remember the years we shared together
tender bitter sweet sending roots deep within
the marrow of my existence the sweet vigilance
of your heart surrounds and lifts me beyond dreams
that I never dared to speak of yet felt
you are the light that shines upon me
lifting shadows of discontent that once
were found in every corner of my world
and as your heaven nears my evening sun
my heart beats with yours my dearest one
finding shelter in your embrace so true
then shall I constant friend all my love renew.

I took a position at a new and exciting mental health program in the Bronx NY, associated with the Albert Einstein College of Medicine. Dr. Jack Wilder was a prominent psychiatrist who promoted the use of day hospitals in the treatment of psychiatric patients. He had received a federal grant to develop this community mental health, or storefront center, in the Bronx. The underlying premise of this program was to combine mental health treatment with social intervention. We focused on the poor and underprivileged people in the area. In addition to active psychiatric intervention, we tried to support various social interventions that would enable our patients to deal with their multiple pressures. It was an exciting time as I explored the social dimensions of psychiatric illness. I learned to provide family and group psychotherapy along with new psychiatric medications. Eventually I became the director of one of the units in the program.

After a few years, I was asked to become the director of The Orange County Mental Health Center in upstate New York. A friend of Dr. Wilder, Jeanne Jonas, was a wealthy patron of Arden Hill Hospital in Goshen NY. She had spearheaded the hospital's attempt to gain federal money for this project. An extension was built to the hospital to provide comprehensive care for mental patients. However, funding had stopped and the building remained empty. I was asked to develop a grant and submit this to the local government agency. Successful in obtaining the necessary funds I began hiring. My new job was exciting and enriching as I continued my clinical work alongside administrative duties. I needed to find staff and develop their clinical skills. I worked with a community board and obtained additional funding. It was a very creative time for me. As director of the entire program, we were able to overcome the barriers that delay and frustrate patients. We had an emergency service, a day hospital, an inpatient unit and an outpatient service. To provide consistency, I directed that the same personnel follow the patient through the entire program. We were able to reduce inpatient stay, provide outpatient follow up and easy re-entry to the hospital. I felt strongly that we needed to develop strong ties to the community we served. Towards that end, I periodically hosted town hall meetings for our patients and the community to discuss our approach and to provide opportunity for feedback. I also arranged for an annual lecture open to the public on various discoveries and treatments in the field of psychiatry. In addition to my clinical and administrative duties there were political tasks as well. Work with the community board required different people-skills that I had to learn along the way. Jeanne's unwavering support and influence in the county was vital to the success of the program. My wife and I developed a warm friendship with Jeanne and her husband, Harold who was Goshen's town historian.

In my fifth year, Dr. Wilder alerted me to an exciting opportunity in Greenwich, Connecticut and I accepted the job as Director of Psychiatry at Greenwich Hospital. I inherited a wonderful staff, which included a psychologist and several social workers. I was the program director but remained active as a clinician. I was often called to the emergency room of the hospital to evaluate someone. I remember seeing one of my Bipolar patients who had become manic and threatening. As I entered the room he was circling like an animal and swinging a rope in a somewhat menacing manner. It seemed to me a message that I should not come closer. He was struggling in his own way to contain his extreme agitation. I was able to calm him down enough that he allowed us to give him the medication he needed and to accept hospitalization. Another man whose drinking had compromised his performance at work became a patient. After several sessions, I suggested that he invite his wife to join us in order to understand their relationship. I do not know exactly how it happened or why it came to be, but this woman saw me as almost a god. I became for her the person who would be there to answer her questions. This lasted long after therapy ended and the couple had moved away. She would call me when she was in trouble and seeing another doctor to make sure she was getting the right medication. She did well in her new surroundings and embarked on an artistic career as a painter. She was a sweet and honest human being. She died soon after and too early. The world lost a pure soul. I had treated another woman for several years for depression and suicidal ideation. She continually argued with me about her future. I would argue back and feel frustrated but there was something about her that was true, needy and warm. She was very dependent on her mother who lived upstairs. I finally convinced Barbara to move to another town. Barbara was quite anxious at first but she adapted and made friends. She soon met and married a man who cherished her. At our last visit, Barbara asked me if I would give her my forwarding address. I hesitated but finally agreed. For the next several years we exchanged Christmas cards.

Semi-retirement and Insights

I turned 65 on June 29, 2000 and decided to retire It was a sad moment but I looked forward to a new stage in my life when we moved to Canada. However, I soon found that I needed to be active clinically. I spent the next few years as an itinerant psychiatrist or 'locum tenens' at various hospitals in upper New York State. Eventually, I took a job for two-and-a-half days a week at the Lewis County Mental Health Center in Lowville, New York, two hours away. The Center was responsible for seriously-ill mental patients. I worked closely with the family doctors in the area who were very caring. However, many of these patients were over-medicated to the point of emotional numbing. I remember one patient who was on 32 different medications. My team included social workers and psychologists. Eventually I became the medical director of the entire program and involved myself in the politics of the county and its mental health board. After several years and with diminishing funding I decided to leave. I had learned of a position opening for a psychiatrist at the Wellness Centre at Queen's University, Kingston, Ontario. I was able to gain a position as a psychiatrist at the Centre on the recommendation of a friend who was its medical director. My first weeks on the job were quite stressful, as I had to prove myself all over again to various observers and regulators. Even though I was a board-certified psychiatrist and a Fellow of the American Psychiatric Association, I had to be strictly supervised by the director of the program, Dr. Stephen McNevin. Luckily for me he was generous with his time. He helped me understand the various requirements peculiar to Canadian medicine and introduced me to various colleagues. Most importantly, he invited me to join the monthly journal club he attended. This became an enormous support throughout my tenure. At first I was uncertain I could help this young student population. I was thrilled to find, despite the age difference, that they responded to me. Over the next seven years I learned much. I carried my own experiences as a patient in analysis seeking relief from unrelenting emotional pain. To my great relief, I was given more freedom to provide extensive therapy. Being young, my patients were not loaded down with medication. I was able to follow quite a few over an extended time until graduation. I also provided group therapy, which proved to be tremendously successful. It was probably the most exciting aspect of my work. *I came to see and understand these extremely bright students who had been stymied by their backgrounds and emotional baggage.* My role was to facilitate their bonding and loosen the ties that strangled their future. This was a group of intelligent and caring young people who were able to identify with each other and claim their own future.

I did not want my prospective patients to regress into total dependency and isolation. I very much described the experience to be a mutual and cooperative endeavor. I emphasized my belief that the past often imprisons us. To my surprise, most seemed to understand what I was trying to offer. Many recounted a history of growing up in a family where the father was distant, harsh, and sometimes punitive. Mothers were often depressed themselves. In turn my patients felt trapped in the recurring cycle of the same issues in their relationships. All wanted freedom from the past but were afraid of the future. After the initial sessions most would agree to a longer commitment to therapy and the hopes of a brighter future. I spent a lot of time describing the process of free association in which he or she could relax enough to speak whatever they saw or felt in the moment. I would try as well to pay close attention to the emotional space between us. I often encouraged an exploration of their dreams. I was an avid dreamer myself and therefore had a kinship with the mysterious imagery of fantasy and emotion. I would also explain that this is no different than how close friends speak with each other. In fact it is the natural order of things for all of us to try and close that gap, to make contact with the inner world and emotional vibration of the other. Frequently patients tried to use language as a barrier to silence and prevent feeling. We would reach a point when it was difficult to move on, an almost dead space between us. My sense would be that there was some anxiety about going deeper coupled with the fear of letting go of the past. It resurrected memories of my own history and struggles. I could identify with their anxiety around this perspective on life.

As we progressed, I tried to remember the emotions and sensitivities inhabiting the previous encounter. This set the tone for my expectations of the current session. In turn, I often asked what they were thinking about or fantasizing as they approached my office. The initial response would be that they were reading a book or thinking about school. Yet I remember well how anxious I felt as I entered my analyst's office. I would try to push them and pay particular attention to the first words they spoke to me. They contained the issues that set the tone for our session. I try to feel the present emotional status of our relationship. Dreams played a big part in our discussions as they expressed their anxieties about establishing this new relationship. I do not try to interpret the dream but rather to allow this expression as a gateway to unconscious anxiety. I found as the dream unfolded, corresponding images and memories would often surface. This often led to a mutual discussion of what is going on in the current life of the individual sitting across from me. *It is comparable to the everyday exchange between good friends.* The difference is that I represent someone new with perhaps a different set of ideas or values. I do not try to convince anyone of my values but rather just to be who I am. As in any good and intense relationship, we are inevitably affected by such an encounter. I have learned much from my patients and they too seem to have grown in the process.

I was surprised when Irene came to my office announcing that this would be the first and last time she would see me. Although she was clearly depressed there was something about her intensity, warmth and intelligence that drew me towards her. She finally agreed to come back and there ensued three years of intensive therapy. She often challenged me but in the context of trust and caring. Her dreams expressed how isolated she had been and how alone she felt. She had a tender heart and needed to be understood. In turn, I cared about her a great deal and realized just how important I was to her. We came to the end of therapy and she graduated to begin her professional life. It was an ending that had to occur. I have not seen or heard from her since but if she needed me I would be there.

In my early years of training, I was supervised closely and submitted detailed notations of the session. There was heavy emphasis on the ability to interpret patient utterances and to confront their neurotic relationships. I did not have to take a detailed inventory of my own responses and intimate feelings. Emphasis was on the verbal back and forth rather than the actual relationship and emotional contact. The primary goal was to be an objective listener unmoved by one's own emotions or conflicts. Yet, as I delved more deeply into Freud's writing, I discovered that he was quite involved with his patients. He had strong beliefs and emotions that he brought to therapy. His gift was his ability to understand himself and his patient as two parts of the same dialogue. My reading of the experiences of Harry Stack Sullivan reinforced this idea of mutuality. He focused on the relationship as the fundamental experience of change. True, that some people only talk about their pain and problems. This certainly has some value. However, I felt and believed that I needed to *unearth what was most precious and most protected.* This led me to understand that I could not be aloof and isolated. I had to connect with my own reveries, my own fears. In short I needed to be a mirror of their own experiences. In many ways, the therapeutic encounter is a piece of theatre, wherein each is playing a role. Patient and therapist bring his or her own past to a present which stretches back to their earliest beginnings. On the surface, the patient tells a story and the therapist listens. Memories and emotions percolate to the surface while each individual listens intently to the gestures of the other. A shrug of the shoulder, a slight smile and most importantly the eyes, offer hints of something mysterious. It is my job as therapist to be sensitive to this ebb and flow and to respond accordingly. This is similar to a good actor's response to the mood and undercurrent of the moment or a jazz musician's improvising to the ambient melody of other musicians. When this occurs, a sense of joy and intimacy creates sparks that flicker between us. The story being told then follows many pathways mingling past and present. As listener, I sense the moment and reflect on my own images and feelings. Much as good friends often do, our conversation goes off in many different directions. *This is the free association of patient and free-floating attention of therapist described by Sigmund Freud.* It becomes the driving force of an intense relationship that changes the perspective of each other's history and values. It also raises significant anxiety around the patient's attachments to internalized parental figures. As in any true relationship, the other profoundly affects us. I have been deeply moved by such encounters with my patients. Their courage and intensity have been remarkable. Their response to me has brought both wonder and joy. As we approach the end of therapy, we discover that each is changed by the experience of the other. In the end it is all about love. Indeed in his papal encyclical, Benedict XV1 wrote: "Deus caritas est. God is love".

Without love, we are left facing the demands of desire and resentment.

Loss

I was an asthmatic child. My earliest memories of my mother centered around my asthma attacks. I would awaken in the night wheezing and. gasping for breath. My mother was always there holding me tight and stroking my back, soothing me. I felt safe though I knew it would take time to regain my regular breathing. I was the oldest in a family of six children five boys and one girl. The early years were relatively warm and stable. I idolized my parents and fought with my younger brother. I was a star at school while he rebelled. Leaving home was something I never would've thought of. I was the curious one especially when it came to health and sex. My parents were especially uncomfortable with these topics and left it up to the family doctor to explain.

As the years went by there seemed to be increasing tension between my mother and father and they eventually slept in different bedrooms. My mother began to drink and my father became more isolated and self-centered. I noticed this especially when I entered high school and a new environment. There, I felt the pull of my fellow students who came from all parts of New York City. This continued throughout my college years. I looked forward while my parents remained stalled and not that interested in what I was doing or reading. They did not come to my graduation from St. Peter's College nor were they there when I got my degree from McGill University College of Medicine, nor to my wedding. The only times I interacted with them was when I worked as a lifeguard at the beach where they had a summer house, and on visits after our children were born.

I recently had a dream in which my father was playing handball with me. It became very tense and I felt uneasy and anxious. My father did actually teach me how to play this sport when I was quite young. He used to hang around with some of the teenage boys I looked up to. With each passing year he became more distant and more critical of me, almost as if I was a threat to him. Meanwhile my mother continued to drink. While my father bridled at my achievements, my mother, with six children to look after, became more anxious about the world in general.

I have realized that twin messages became embedded in my inner world.

At each stage of my life, I welcomed challenges successfully. However, those inner messages from my youth instilled a lifelong anxiety. I realize that I have never quite left my parents. They live in my inner world, clinging to the past and its dangers. The child within remains a constant refrain that I resent. I have always thought that my father's belittlement was paramount. Yet I now understand that my mother's fear of the world also remains with me though hidden in the dark corners of my mind. When I search for an outward threat, the image of my father and his rejection surfaces. When I sense uncertainty and increasing anxiety something of my mother's anxious eyes take hold of me and I retreat. As I grew towards adolescence and adventure, my mother issued warnings. She was particularly wary of my going to the nearby park and outdoor athletic center. I would go there with my friends to play basketball or roller hockey. She was afraid that someone would do me harm. I tried to assure her that I was particularly safe with my friends and could easily walk home a few blocks. I could see the anguish in her face as I would walk out the door. She remained a mother hen, constantly keeping her fold near her. Despite her warnings and fear, her children left for far away places, in search of fulfillment in California, Florida, Maryland, Puerto Rico, Canada and Switzerland.

The Other

On meeting someone, I hope for signs of connection, a sense of warmth, intelligence and acceptance. This has resulted in a lonely existence as most people protect themselves from even a hint of intimacy. It is probably the reason that I chose psychiatry and especially psychotherapy. Under these circumstances, my patients, though hesitant, are also searching for intimacy and healing; they are bravely open to dialogue even with their emotional pain and vulnerability at stake. The therapeutic environment offers a bubble of safety within the challenge to open up the wounds of childhood and fears of rejection. This takes me back to my own experiences and struggles for freedom.

Marriage has been the platform for me to open and expand myself to the woman I love. She has been the one constant in my life, confronting my hesitancy and retreat into myself even as she exposes her own fears. I marvel at her love for me and the challenge this presents. My initial response is wonder. This forces me to move on and to share my love for her. I find that as we come together my universe expands and the world seems friendly and supportive. At the same time, I am more confident and more aware of the need to support her, to guide her, to believe in her, to become one with her as we face the world together.

Love

When I was young, the world seemed large and forbidding

I retreated to an inner world filled with desire

Love was a fantasy shrouded with fear

Friendships came and went whimsically

God was an avenging angel seeking revenge

On the pleasures that called in the distance

Then you sought me out ever so quietly that

I hardly knew. You were gentle with me and patient

As you surrounded me with love. You seemed to need me

And understood who I was. Your gift quelled the demons and lifted

My spirit to your world my dearest one. As we

Looked forward to the morning sun.

Afterword

My earliest years were full of anguish and neurotic fears. I cannot pinpoint the exact time it all began but it was around the time I was able to read at elementary school. On my walk to school, I remember avoiding certain streets that seemed to suggest danger, a threat of danger reinforced by the strict and demanding nuns who controlled and taught us in our grade school. These nuns described a fearful world in which we might all be eternally damned. I had come from an idyllic nursery school and a magical teacher to the shock of my first grade which was taught by an elderly nun whose vision of life was one of unending doom and terrifying demons. My anguish there was further reinforced by an Irish Catholicism dominated by puritanical ideas. In those days I would repeatedly go to the confessional to recite my sinful thoughts. The priests were understanding and thoughtful but nevertheless, my fear of sexuality and its ultimate damnation stayed with me.

I graduated from grade school to enter a distinguished all-boy-school Catholic high school in Manhattan where every student gained admission by scholarship after passing a difficult entrance examination. The students came from all parts of New York City and seemed to be intelligent. It took me an hour by train from Brooklyn to get to Regis at 85th St. and Park Avenue. I played varsity sports and won letters in swimming, baseball and tennis while working hard to maintain high grades. Now, entering my teens, my imagination soared as my sexual drive increased. Weekends I went to Friday night dances in my parish as well as popular musicals in Manhattan. These experiences intensified my thoughts and imagination. It bought me to frequent meetings with a kind and gentle father-confessor at my school. He reassured me, yet I remained conflicted. My summers at our beach house where I was a lifeguard just intensified these conflicts.

After Regis, I received a scholarship to a Jesuit college where I reached the top of my class. During the next four years I had many opportunities to meet young girls yet remained distant and emotionally constrained. I went on to McGill University School of Medicine in Montreal. This was an important period of growth where I made new friends and managed to leave behind some of the stifling religious struggles of my childhood. I did well in my studies in medical school and went on to an internship and residency in psychiatry at St. Vincent's Hospital in New York City. This brought new friendships as well as new challenges. The young nurses at the hospital were friendly and available. Here again I could get only so close to someone before retreating. My shyness did not go away.

This pattern continued when I joined the United States Army and went off to the war in Vietnam. Although it was also a time of growth, I remained hesitant. While stationed in Saigon, now Ho Chi Minh City, I worked at an Army hospital as a psychiatrist treating support troops who worked and fought behind the front lines. There I also made new friends but remained distant.

When I returned from Vietnam and a new life, I vowed to gain some measure of freedom. To address my demons, I decided to set enter psychoanalysis. It was a time when I had frequent dreams with disturbing images full of water, threatening figures hammering my soul. At times I felt I was drowning. This was my secret life that I never shared except for the hours I spent on the couch. As time went by, my dreams soared to heights I never knew possible. Eventually, I felt comfortable challenging my analyst who was encouraging while remaining distant. I ended therapy with mixed feelings recognizing his help yet resenting this distance.

Although I managed to navigate my life as an adult, including the danger in a war, I was not completely free of anxious tendencies and the fear of dying a terrible death. These fears were companions to my sexual life and the need to relate to someone. Throughout these years, I immersed myself in the study of philosophy and theology hoping to gain some freedom. Somehow, I was able to marry, maintain the love of my life and have children. I struggle with all my might not to fail the people I love.

My years as a psychiatrist brought profound enrichment and engagement with the world. My sessions with patients seemed to be a magical bubble that was completely safe. In this capacity, I could use my imagination as a bridge to that person looking for a truth that would offer freedom. It was a not so much that I had any specific knowledge and understanding. Rather the sessions became a fulfilling relationship that struck at the heart of anxiety. I have received extraordinary letters from several of my former patients thanking me for guiding them to a better life and confidence in the future. These letters always took me by surprise. They touched me deeply and reinforced my belief that life has meaning.

Postscript

Near an aging forest, there is a verdant field
undulating beneath a sun that never sets.
Far off in a corner of this field,
a man emerges from the lip of a dark tunnel.
He blinks, his eyes unused to such bright light
and he slowly, unsteadily, raises himself to his full height.
The look on his face describes pain and determination,
mixed with sadness.
It is obvious that he is glad to be in this field
but has left something or someone dear to him behind.
As he walks forward his gait falters
as if caught or tugged at but he moves on intently
and with more forceful stride.
The beauty of the day and the hills and the field
is overwhelmingly joyful.
He cocks an ear expectantly
for the land invites the feeling of life.
Yet there is no sound.
He is alone and frightened
but walks on singing to himself
as God whispers through the trees.

– William Kenny

Bibliography

1. Jaspers, Karl (2003), *Way to Wisdom An Introduction to Philosophy* Yale University Press, New Haven, London

2. Sullivan, H.S. (1953) *The Interpersonal Theory of Psychiatry*, Norton, N Y 1953

3. Fairbairn, Ronald (1994), *From Instinct to Self, Selected Papers*, Ed. Elinor Fairbairn Jason Aronson Northvale NJ, London

4. Green, André (1986), *A Private Madness,*
   The Dead Mothe,r pp. 142-173 Hogarth Press ,London

5 Bollas, Christopher (1989), *The Shadow of the Object: Psychoanalysis of the Unthought Known:* Columbia University Press NY

6. Lee, Ronald R, Martin V Colby (1991), *Psychotherapy After Kohut* The Atlantic Press, Hillsdale NY

7. Jemstedt, Arne & Phillips, Adam ed. (2011),*The Christopher Bollas Reader*, ch16: "The Wisdom of the Dream" 249-258 Routledge NY, London

8. Meares, Russell WW (1993) *The Metaphor of Play.* Jason Aronson, Northvale NJ , London

9. Bollas, Christpopher(1989), *The Forces of Destiny* , ch10: "Don't Worry About Your Father" pg 181-199 Jason Aranson NJ, Londo

10. Shore, Allan N (2012), *The Science of the Art of Psychotherapy,* Ch4: The Right Brain Implicit Self Lies at the Core of Psychoanalysis pp 118-143 WW Norton NY, London

11. Atwood G & Stolorow R (1984), *Structures of Subjectivity: Explorations in Psychoanalytic Phenomenology,* p34 The Analytic Press Hillsdale NJ, London

12. Lee, Ronald & Martin, J Colby (1991*), A Textbook of Self Psychology,* The Analytic Press, Hillsdale NJ, London

13. May,Rollo (1969), *Love and Will* Ch 8 "Wish and Will" pp207-208: WW Norton N15

14. Grotstein James S (2004), *Notes on the Superego Psychoanalytic Inquiry* Vol 24, issue 2 pg 257-270

15 Jemstead,Arne &Phillips, Adam ed (201i), *The Christopher Bollas Reader*,Ch12 "Creativity and Psychoanalysis" pp.194-206, Routledge, NY, Londo

16. Meissner WW (1991 , *What is Effective in Psychoanalytic Psychotherapy*, Jason Aronson , Northvale NJ ,London

17. Andreasen Nancy C (2014) "The Secrets of the Creative Brain", *The Atlantic Monthly* July /August 2014 pp. 62-75

18. Appignanesi,Lisa & Forrester, John, (1992) *Freud's Women* Weidenfeld &Nicolsen, Great Britain

Deus Caritas Est : Benedict XV1 Papal Encyclical 2005

The Cambridge Companion to Freud- Neu. Terrence Cambridge 1991

Reverie and Interpretation: Ogden, Thomas Routledge N Y 2018

Psychoanalysis Never Lets Go: Roustang, Francois Johns Hopkins Press 1983

Symbol and Meaning in Psychoanalytic Psychotherapy
Encounter, Gesture and Fantasy

November 17, 2009
Lewis County Community Mental Health Center

William F. Kenny MD

Readings

Michael Balint	Basic Fault
Martin Buber	I and Thou
Ronald Fairbairn	From Instinct to Self
Anna Freud	Ego and Mechanisms of Defense
Sigmund Freud	Studies on Hysteria Analysis Terminable and Interminable
Karl Jaspers	Reason and Existenz
David Johnston	Transference and Counter Transference And Jungian Depth Therapy
Otto Kernberg	Psychotherapy of the Borderline Patient
Frederick Morton	A Nervous Splendor
Paul Ricoeur	Freud and Philosophy
Francois Roustang	Psychoanalysis Never Lets Go
Harry Stack Sullivan	The Interpersonal Theory of Psychiatry

www.ingramcontent.com/pod-product-compliance
Lightning Source LLC
Chambersburg PA
CBHW051627140626
46547CB00033B/2770